TREES
FOR
HEALING

By the same authors:

THE NEWCASTLE GUIDE TO HEALING WITH CRYSTALS:
Balancing the Human Energy System for Physical and
Spiritual Well-Being

THE NEWCASTLE GUIDE TO HEALING WITH GEMSTONES:
How to Use Over 70 Different Energies

TREES FOR HEALING

Harmonizing With Nature
for
Personal Growth and Planetary Balance

PAMELA LOUISE CHASE
and
JONATHAN PAWLIK

NEWCASTLE PUBLISHING CO., INC.
North Hollywood, California
1991

Edited by James Strohecker and Nancy Shaw Strohecker
Copyedited by Ann McCarthy
Cover Design by Michele Lanci-Altomare
Cover photography of Interior Live Oak by Michele Lanci-Altomare
Illustrations:

    Aymalee: Chapter 6—Jennifer and the Little Fir, pp. 47, 48, 49, 51, 52, 53, 54, 243.

    Shephard C. Brookes & Byron P. Howard: Figs. 2-12, 2-13, 2-14, 2-15; pp. 11, 12, 13, 14, 97, 99, 101, 107, 111, 113, 147, 205, 209, 212, 215, 217.

Grateful acknowledgment is made to the following for permission to reprint copyrighted material:

    J.M. Francis, artist.
    Commonwealth of Pa: *Common Trees of Pennsylvania*, by the Department of Environmental Resources, Copyright 1971 by the Commonwealth of Pa.
    Figs. 2-1, 2-2, 2-3, 2-4, 2-5, 2-6, 2-7, 2-10, 2-11; pp. 9, 10, 125, 134, 141, 143, 145, 149, 152, 154, 156, 158, 162, 164, 166, 168, 170, 172, 174, 176, 179, 182, 184, 186, 188, 190, 194, 198, 200, 207.

    Carole Kahler, artist.
    Olympic Branch, Pacific Northwest National Parks and Forests Association in cooperation with the Olympic National Park: *Everchanging Evergreen, the Lowland Forests of Olympic National Park*, revised, Copyright 1984 by the Pacific Northwest National Parks and Forests Association. pp. 74, 79, 85, 88, 90.

    American Forestry Association: *Trees Every Boy and Girl Should Know*, by the Bureau of Forestry, Copyright 1968 by the American Forestry Association.
    Figs. 2-8, 2-9; pp. 10, 72, 76, 81, 83, 92, 95, 103, 105, 109, 117, 119, 121, 123, 128, 130, 132, 136, 139, 160, 192, 196, 202.

    Jan Salerno, artist.
    St. Martin's Press: *The Book of Runes*, by Ralph Blum, Copyright 1987 by St. Martin's Press.
    p. 16.

DISCLAIMER

    This book is not intended to diagnose, prescribe, or treat any ailment, nor is it intended in any way as a replacement for medical consultation when needed. The author and publishers of this book do not guarantee the efficacy of any of the methods herein described, and strongly suggest that at the first suspicion of any disease or disorder the reader consult a physician.

First Edition April 1991

A Newcastle Book
First Printing April 1991
9 8 7 6 5 4 3 2 1
Printed in the United States of America on Recycled Paper

ACKNOWLEDGMENTS

We wish to thank the people at Newcastle Publishing and especially our editors James Strohecker and Nancy Shaw Strohecker for their enthusiasm and hard work, and their sensitive and skillful editing.

We also thank Aymalee, Shephard C. Brookes and Byron P. Howard for their beautiful artwork and their support of our project.

Finally we extend our love to the trees who continue to teach us with infinite patience and understanding.

CONTENTS

LIST OF ILLUSTRATIONS

PART ONE

Exploring the Tree Kingdom

In Part I, we discuss getting to know the trees, first from a physical perspective, and then from a spiritual perspective. It is important to remember that spiritual perceptions are determined by our belief systems, and by how we receive our intuitive information. Therefore we are describing our reality as we perceive it. We share our perceptions with you in order to open further possibilities for you to explore on your own spiritual path.

Chapter Six is a children's story, called "Jennifer and the Little Fir." If you have children you can share it with them. You can also allow your own Inner Child to enjoy its childlike innocence, for this is a key to appreciating Nature.

1 | Trees— Our Precious Resource

As scientists, many of us have had profound experiences of awe and reverence before the universe. We understand that what is regarded as sacred is more likely to be treated with care and respect. Our planetary home should be so regarded.[1]

—Carl Sagan

THE HEALING OF our planet is occurring on both the personal and global level today. Mother Earth is teaching both societies and individuals that we must change our values and behavior, and that we cannot continue to exist through selfishness and greed. If we do not learn to care for our physical home, the Earth, we will destroy it.

Scientists have shown us that we are living at a critical time that calls for some far-reaching choices. Climate experts agree that the build-up of carbon dioxide in the atmosphere is leading to the greenhouse effect, disruptive weather patterns, crop losses, and dramatic climatic changes. Trees have been the principle mechanism in nature for maintaining the proper carbon dioxide balance. As the chloroplasts in the leaves use the carbon in the air to make sugars and starches, they release the leftover oxygen back into the air. With the excessive destruction of the forest cover in this century, the delicate balance between oxygen and carbon dioxide in the atmosphere has been disrupted.

Just over a thousand years ago, some ninety percent of the earth's land was still covered with forest. By the year 1900 only twenty percent of the land remained forested. Our forests are disappearing for a number of reasons. One is the weakening health of our trees. There are a number of people who think that the lack of necessary minerals in our soil contributes to the trees' susceptibility to environmental pollution. It is known that our trees are being watered by acid rain, which is a by-product of the burning of fossil fuels. Disease and insect damage are signs of unhealthy soil and plants. Blights such as the Dutch Elm disease have begun to take a heavy toll only in the past fifty to one hundred years. Various insect populations such as the gypsy moth have also increased tree damage, and chemical poisons have proved largely ineffective. Parts of our forests are being consumed by fires spread by the unusually dry and cold weather patterns. The death and destruction of these trees is serving as a warning that we must correct the way we treat our environment.

The other major cause of tree devastation has been the continual increase of timber cutting. Each year almost three billion trees, or an area of forest about the size of England, is destroyed, mostly in the tropics. The Rainforest Action Network has reported that many of these trees are destroyed in order to raise beef cattle for fast-food chains in this country. The Foundation of Economic Trends in Washington, D.C. estimates that every quarter-pound hamburger containing beef from the rainforest represents the destruction of fifty-five square feet of tropical trees. That destruction in turn causes the emission of five hundred pounds of carbon dioxide into the atmosphere per hamburger.

Local governments are also destroying the rainforests in the process of trying to "catch up" with the industrialized nations. They are building new settlements, clearing land for agriculture, and building dams that drown billions of trees. "Greed and gross political and economic inequalities are much more serious causes of the destruction of the world's rainforests than increasing population."[2]

It seems that we have tended to assume that there are an unlimited number of trees that exist for the purpose of convenient consumption. It now takes a one-hundred-foot-tall tree to provide the wood and paper products consumed annually by the average American. However, many of these wood and paper products are unnecessarily wasted rather than recycled.

Nearly four hundred years ago the colonists arrived in our coun-

try to live in 850,000,000 acres of virgin forest. Now, other than protected national parks and wilderness areas, the untouched woods
amount to about one million scattered acres. President Theodore
Roosevelt was one of the far-sighted politicians who saw the need for
the conservation of our forests. In 1905 he established the national
forest system with 148,000,000 acres of forest in trust. These forests
remained essentially uncut for fifty years or so, until the Forest Service yielded to the increasing demand for lumber. In 1989 the Forest
Service allowed sixty thousand acres of old growth forest to be cut.
According to some conservationists' estimates, cutting at this rate
could deplete the old growth forests in fifteen years. On a global
level, forests are being cut at the rate of seventy-five acres per
minute, or five thousand square miles a month.

The controversy over the extinction of the spotted owl in the
old growth forests of Oregon and Washington is complicated by the
fact that the Japanese are currently offering twice the amount of
money that American mills can pay for old growth logs. Timber cutting on private lands of the large timber companies has increased to
take advantage of the profits.

Reforestation projects by lumber companies typically consist of
large plantings of a single species for the continued commercial purposes of producing pulpwood and other products for industry. These
are not balanced ecological systems and therefore do not contribute
to the well-being of other species and our planet as a whole. Many
industrialized nations practice "whole tree harvesting" where the
branches and leaves are removed and the area is burned, depleting
topsoil and leaving the area exposed to erosion and flooding, not to
mention the loss of other animal and plant life. In our society we
need to revise our view of trees as being more than a commodity for
human consumption. We hope that this book will provide the kind
of information and experiences that will bring about changes in attitudes and behavior which will promote the healthy life of our
planet.

Two promising approaches to solving the problems of deforesta-
tion and the greenhouse effect are remineralization of the soil with
rock dust and the planting of billions of trees.

John Hamaker is the principal proponent of remineralizing the
forests with rock dust ground up from glacial gravel. According to
Hamaker glaciers naturally remineralize the soil by crushing rocks
and gravel into fine dust. Rock dust is then carried by the wind to
other areas of the Earth's land surface that are not covered by ice

sheets, effectively remineralizing the Earth. Glacial rock is rich in important trace minerals as well as the nitrogen, phosphorus and potash that are needed for growth. Remineralization also strengthens the trees against disease, insects, and harsh climatic changes.

A number of people have demonstrated the success of remineralization. One of them is Rudolf Schindele in Grimsing, Austria. Schindele owned some woods in the Black Forest where many evergreens were dying. He decided to build some logging roads through his woods, and realized that the rock dust from his road work was rehabilitating the trees where the wind had scattered the dust. In 1987 Schindele built a large mill for grinding the paragneiss rock dust. He now exports rock dust all over the world for reforestation and agricultural projects. Remineralization with rock dust has also been used successfully in Germany and Australia.

Hamaker and others have seen the need to plant billions of trees. Over twenty years ago in Los Angeles, Andy Lipkis founded TreePeople, an organization responsible for the planting of more than two hundred million trees. One of Lipkis' projects has been the distribution of discarded nursery fruit trees to the poor. One of his goals is to create "villages" in Los Angeles where the local people plant and maintain trees. The American Forestry Association has a similar project called the Global Releaf Program. This program supports groups that plant trees.

There are tree-planting projects that cater to the needs of the local communities that must care for them. In the hill areas of Choluteca, Honduras, areas that were cut over fifty years ago, are now being planted with cashew trees and harvested by local cooperatives. The cashews are harvested with low investment and labor-intensive methods that allow local people a greater measure of control over their lives and the quality of their environment.

You might be wondering, "How can I participate and make a difference?" The first step we can make is to deepen our understanding of our connection to Nature. This is most eloquently illustrated by the words of Chief Seattle in his message to President Franklin Pierce in 1854 before turning his lands over to the federal government:

> We are part of the earth and it is part of us.
> The perfumed flowers are our sisters;
> the deer, the horse, the great eagle,
> these are our brothers.

The rocky crests, the juices of the meadows,
the body heat of the pony, and man—
all belong to the same family.

So when the Great Chief in Washington sends word
that he wishes to buy our land, he asks much of us . . .

If we decide to accept, I will make one condition:
The white man must treat the beasts of this land
as his brothers.
I am a savage and do not understand any other way.

I have seen a thousand rotting buffalos on the prairie,
left by the white man who shot them from a passing train.
I am a savage and I do not understand how the smoking
iron horse can be more important than the buffalo
that we kill only to stay alive.

Where is man without the beasts?
If the beasts were gone, men would die
from a great loneliness of spirit.
For whatever happens to the beasts soon happens to man.
All things are connected.
This we know.
The earth does not belong to man;
man belongs to the earth.
This we know.

All things are connected,
like the blood which unites one family.
All things are connected.
Whatever befalls the earth befalls the sons of the earth.

Man did not weave the web of life,
he is merely a strand in it.
Whatever he does to the web,
he does to himself.[3]

2 | Physical Roots—
The Tree Kingdom

TREE IDENTIFICATION

IN ORDER TO identify a tree, it helps to know some questions to ask, as well as how trees are commonly described. Trees are usually divided into three groups: *broadleaved trees, conifers,* and *tropical trees.*

The broadleaved trees beautify large areas of Europe and North America with their thin, flat leaves. These trees produce flowers, and after pollination these flowers develop seeds. In order to survive the temperate climate winters, most broadleaved trees are *deciduous,* that is, they shed their leaves in autumn and become dormant until spring. There is a small group of broadleaved evergreens, such as Southern Magnolia and Pacific Madrone, that keep their leaves all year around. Their thick, glossy leaves are a protection against cold and dry weather.

For identification purposes, the leaves of broadleaved trees can be divided into two types: *simple* and *compound.* A simple leaf is joined by its stalk to a woody twig. If you pull a leaf off its twig, it will leave a distinct scar. However, the leaflet of a compound leaf is attached to a flexible "midrib," and when you pluck a leaflet, it does not leave a scar.

| Quaking Aspen | Red Maple | Shagbark Hickory | Black Walnut |

FIGURE 2-1. Simple Leaves   FIGURE 2-2. Compound Leaves

While you are looking at the leaves on the trees, there are several things to notice. First of all, are the edges of the leaves *toothed* or *lobed*?

Yellow Birch   White Oak

FIGURE 2-3. Toothed Leaves   FIGURE 2-4. Lobed Leaves

Do the leaves occur in *opposite* pairs, or do they *alternate* on the twig?

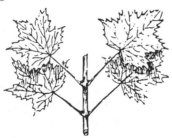

Sugar Maple   Yellow Birch

FIGURE 2-5. Opposite Leaves   FIGURE 2-6. Alternate Leaves

The needles and scales of conifers are well adapted to the colder climates where they are most often found. Pine needles, for example, have a thick outer layer that is coated with wax, to reduce water loss. The sloping branches of the firs shed snow easily, and the needles have a built-in antifreeze to help them survive the cold. When you look at conifers, notice whether they have *needles* (pines, spruces, firs) or *scales* (cypresses, cedars).

Red Spruce

FIGURE 2-7. Conifer Needles

Western Red Cedar

FIGURE 2-8. Conifer Scales

Are the needles in *clusters,* and if so, how many in a cluster? If the needles grow singly on a twig, are they *sharp* or *blunt* on the end?

Lodgepole Pine

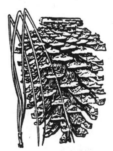

Loblolly Pine

Eastern White Pine

FIGURE 2-9. Needles in Clusters

Norway Spruce

FIGURE 2-10. Sharp Needles

Eastern Hemlock

FIGURE 2-11. Blunt Needles

HOW TREES GROW

In all growth, an ending becomes a beginning, because growth is circular rather than linear. To understand how seeds are produced and how a tree grows from those seeds, we must begin with a culmination of a tree's growth—the flower. On many trees the flower usually has a male and a female part. The female part is the *pistil*, which has a ball-shaped base and a slender neck. Around the pistil are the male parts, called *stamens*, which are like thin stalks that are topped by *anthers*.

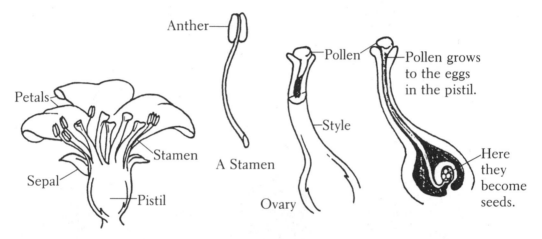

FIGURE 2–12. Parts of a Flower

The anthers produce pollen, which is carried by wind or by insects to the pistils. Many female flowers, whose pollen is brought by the wind, trap the pollen with the sticky tips of their pistils. The male flowers, containing stamens and anthers, may hang in tassels that shake their pollen into the air. Female flowers, who receive pollen from busy insects, rely on their bright colors or sweet scent to attract these insects.

There is a lot of variety in the types of tree flowers. The flowers on dogwoods and tulip trees produce both eggs and pollen, so the pollen doesn't travel very far. However, the flowers on sugar maples, oaks, and hickories are either male or female on the same tree. In a few trees such as the gingko and the Pacific madrone, the tree produces only male or female flowers. A pine tree creates its male flowers in small slender cones. The female cones are shorter and thicker, and the eggs are hidden under the scales.

Once the pollen reaches the pistil, each pollen cell sends out a tube, which unites with the egg cells in the base of the pistil, and a seed is created. The pistil may then become a protective casing for the seed, such as a fruit or a nut.

These seeds inside their casings are spread in much the same ways as pollen. Willow seeds for example are tufted, so that they will float in the wind. Maple seeds have "wings," and they twirl and dance as they are swept away. Birds and animals scatter seeds by eating fruits and nuts, and passing the seeds as droppings. Only a few of the thousands of seeds created will find a friendly home in which to germinate.

Big Leaf Maple   Black Willow   White Oak

FIGURE 2–13. Seeds and Casings

Each tiny seed contains the beginning of a root and a stem. They are covered by special leaves that store food called *cotyledons*. The yearly growth cycle begins with the roots. Each root grows millions of hairs that absorb moisture from the soil. The roots grow longer each year when the cells in the tip of each root begin to divide in the spring. Some cells lengthen the root. Other cells divide and form a protective cap over the root as it grows. The roots become a crisscrossed anchor for the tree. A tree that is 165 feet tall might have roots that would cover an area the size of a football field.

The cells of the stem of a little seedling eventually differentiate into parts of the trunk. The bark of the tree protects it from insects and weather. Under the inner bark is a thin, white layer called the *cambium*. The inner part of the cambium builds the sapwood and the outer part makes new bark. This is how the tree grows fatter.

The growth rings or annual rings that you see at the cut end of a log show how much wood the cambium has made each year. Each growth ring has a thick part and a thin part. The thick part is made in the spring when the trees grow most rapidly. The thinner part is made in the summer and the fall. Thinner annual rings indicate a dry or a cool growing season. Trees that grow rapidly have growth rings that are closer together and therefore harder to see. You can approximate the age of a tree by counting the growth rings.

The sapwood is under the cambium, and in young trees, most of the wood is sapwood. The sapwood is filled with many tiny tubes carrying sap. Water comes into the roots and is changed into sap, which then travels up the tubes to the leaves. The leaves exchange water and minerals for a sugary material that serves as food for the rest of the tree. This sugary substance is manufactured by *chlorophyll*, a green pigment that serves as a catalyst in the process of *photosynthesis*. In this process, carbon dioxide, water, and sunlight are combined to form a sugar. This sugary material is then carried through the sapwood tubes to all parts of the tree.

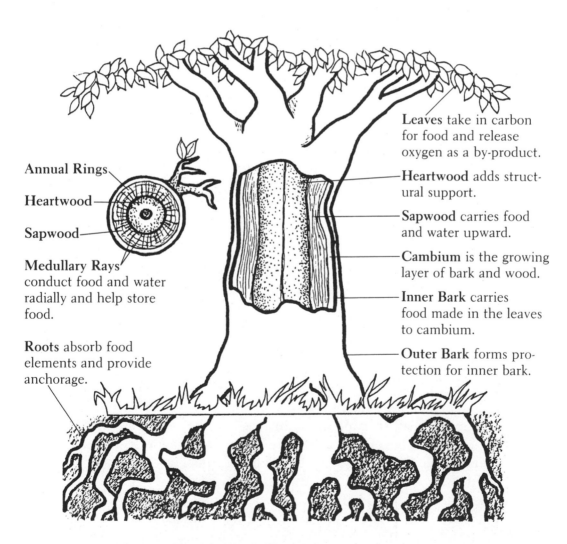

Annual Rings

Heartwood

Sapwood

Medullary Rays conduct food and water radially and help store food.

Roots absorb food elements and provide anchorage.

Leaves take in carbon for food and release oxygen as a by-product.

Heartwood adds structural support.

Sapwood carries food and water upward.

Cambium is the growing layer of bark and wood.

Inner Bark carries food made in the leaves to cambium.

Outer Bark forms protection for inner bark.

FIGURE 2–14. Different Parts of a Tree

We know that the tree grows fatter through the work of the cambium. The branches grow longer in the following manner. At the tip of the twig is a group of specialized cells called the *end bud*. When these cells divide the twig grows longer. The newest growth is separated from the previous year's growth by a series of encircling end bud scars. You can identify a tree in winter by studying the end buds and the end bud scars.

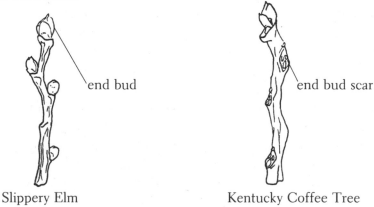

Slippery Elm   Kentucky Coffee Tree

FIGURE 2–15. End Buds and End Bud Scars

When autumn comes, the tree prepares for dormancy and for next year's growth. The spring growth of root hairs dies, and the roots themselves store food to send up through the sapwood in the coming spring.

As the chlorophyll decomposes in deciduous trees, the leaves begin to change color. This process of changing color is still not completely understood. In the warm months the tree produces chlorophyll which is green. The trees that turn yellow in the fall also produce other pigments such as the carotene in carrots and xanthophyll in egg yolks. When the chlorophyll disintegrates, these yellow pigments that were present all summer, become visible.

The red colors are produced by added pigments, the anthocyanins. The anthocyanins are carried in solution in the tree's sap. The production of anthocyanins is an inherited ability, which is why some trees, such as sugar maples, will turn red, and other trees, such as birches, almost never turn red. Other factors that favor the development of the red pigment are the amount of sunshine a leaf receives, and the amount of sugar in the leaf. When all these factors are present and the temperature drops below forty-five degrees Fahrenheit, more sugar remains in the leaf and the anthocyanins accumulate in the sap in the leaves. We then see the glowing scarlet of the scarlet oaks, the gentle crimson of the dogwoods, and the brilliant reds of the red and sugar maples.

In the deciduous trees that change color, the tiny sap tubes in the stems begin to close, and when they are all closed, the leaf falls. The leaf scars are distinctive and a tree can be identified in the winter by studying the leaf scars, as well as the bud scars. Conifers and broadleaf evergreens will lose a few leaves each year rather than losing their leaves all at once like the deciduous trees.

In autumn we also see the development of the leaf and flower buds. Often the end buds will hold tiny flowers and the side buds will become tiny leaves. The flower buds will usually be a different shape from the leaf buds. However, some trees will grow their leaves and flowers in the same bud. With the production of the buds, we are once again at a place of endings and beginnings. The seeds, flowers, leaves, and buds are the individual signatures of living beings involved in the process of birth and rebirth, providing us with lessons in the continuity of change, and the will toward growth.

Odin on the Yggdrasil,
or World Tree,
Spies the Runes

3 | Spiritual Roots— The Sacred Tree in History and Mythology

ANCIENT PEOPLES lived according to the cycles of the seasons and many recognized the presence of spirit in all living things. The physical structure of the tree stood as a divine expression of how the endless diversity of life grows from a single seed. In many cultures the tree is regarded as a source of spiritual wisdom and thus given prominence.

In India, Buddha received enlightenment under the bodhi tree, the tree of the "Waking to Omniscience." The suggestion is that one should contemplate the wisdom found under this tree, and find the way to eliminate suffering through releasing desire and fear.

In the Old Norse Poetic Edda, the All-Father was said to have created the Ash tree of the Universe called Yggdrasil, which symbolized life, time and destiny. The name *Yggdrasil* means "steed of Odin." In Norse mythology, Odin hung on this tree for nine days to gain the wisdom of the Runes. Odin says,

> I know I hung on that windswept tree,
> Swung there for nine long nights,
> Wounded by my own blade,
> Bloodied for Odin,
> Myself an offering to myself:

17

> Bound to the tree
> That no man knows
> Whither the roots of it run.[1]

The idea of an inverted tree of wisdom with its roots above first appeared in the Indian *Katha Upanishad*:

> Root above, branches below. This primal fig tree!
> Pure indeed its root: it is brahman, known
>   as the immortal.
> In it rests all the worlds:
> No one soever goes beyond it.
> All this verily in that tree.[2]

The spiritual wisdom of the inverted tree appears again as the Tree of Sephiroth, in the Kabbalah. The Kabbalah is a record of the secret philosophies of Chasidism, a mystical branch of Judaism. In the Zohar, the chief medieval text of the Kabbalah (written approximately A.D. 1280), creation was described as a tree with its roots in the reality of spirit and its branches in the illusion of physical existence. This tree, called "The Tree of Sephiroth," was therefore inverted, to show its roots in heaven and its branches upon the earth. It was meant to teach that while the growth on the physical plane is outward and expansive, the growth of inner knowing is inward, toward the center. The inverted tree thus grows inward toward its own seed, until at last the physical and the spiritual worlds are joined.

The tree as a source of wisdom is also depicted in art and legend as the "axial tree" or the center upon which the earth revolves. The Greeks, Persians, Chaldeans, and Japanese all have legends describing the axial tree. Thomas Carlyle, a nineteenth-century British historian, wrote:

> I like too that representation they have of the Tree Igdrasil. All Life is figured by them as a Tree. Igdrasil, the Ash-tree of existence, has its roots deep-down in the kingdoms of Death; its trunk reaches up heaven-high, spreads its boughs over the whole Universe: it is the Tree of Existence. At the foot of it, in the Death-kingdom, sit the three Fates—the Past, Present, and Future; watering its roots from the Sacred Well. Its "bough," with their buddings and disleafings,—events, things suffered, things done, catastrophes,—stretch through all lands and times. Is not every leaf of it a biography, every fiber there an act or word? Its boughs are Histories of Nations. The rustle of it is the

noise of Human Existence, onwards from of old. It grows there, the breath of Human Passion rustling through it;—or stormtost, the stormwind howling through it like the voice of all the gods. It is Igdrasil, the Tree of Existence. It is the past, the present, and the future; what was done, what is doing, what will be done; the infinite conjugation of the verb To do . . . I find no similitude so true as this of a Tree. Beautiful; altogether beautiful and great.[3]

A vision of the axial tree is described by Black Elk, the last keeper of the Sacred Pipe of the Oglala Sioux Indians. This vision took place in 1872 as Black Elk stood on Harney Peak in the Black Hills of South Dakota:

I was standing on the highest mountain of them all, and round about beneath me was the whole hoop of the world. And while I stood there I saw more than I can tell and I understood more than I saw; for I was seeing in a sacred manner the shapes of all things in the spirit, and the shape of all shapes as they must live together like one being. And I saw that the sacred hoop of my people was one of the many hoops that made one circle, wide as the daylight and as starlight, and in the center grew one mighty flowering tree to shelter all the children of one mother and one father. And I saw that it was holy.[4]

Trees as a source of spiritual wisdom also appear in the Bible in Genesis, as The Tree of Life and the Tree of Knowledge of Good and Evil. The Kabbalists see The Tree of Life as representing the spiritual point of balance—the secret of immortality. The Tree of Knowledge of Good and Evil represents the polarity of physical existence, or the secret of mortality. In the Tree of Sephiroth, the Kabbalists made the Tree of Life the central column, and The Tree of Knowledge of Good and Evil the two side trunks.

TREE WORSHIP: THE SACRED TREE

Throughout the ancient world, trees were thought to be animate, with souls like our own. Thus they were worshipped as proxies of Divinity, with attributes of divine power and intelligence. The oracular oaks of the ancient Greek world were a well-known example of this worship. The worship of Apollo included the establishment of places of prophecy so that the gods could communicate with humankind. The oldest place of prophecy was the place of the "talking oak" trees, the oracle of Dodona. These trees stood together to form a sacred grove. When the priests wanted answers, they went to the grove after purifying themselves, and the trees spoke with the voices of human beings. Some say that Zeus inhabited one particular oak tree, which became known as "the oracular oak."

Jupiter was the Roman counterpart to the Greek Zeus and was later revered at "the oracular oak." Zeus and Jupiter were the gods of sky, rain, and thunder. It was said that thunderstorms raged at Dodona more frequently than at any other place in ancient Greece.

It is fascinating to note that in the ancient German sacred rituals, the oak was also dedicated to the god of thunder, Donar or Thunar, the equivalent of the Norse Thor. The ancient Slavs also had a thunder god, Perun, to whom the oak tree was sacred. Thus among the ancient Teutons and Slavs, as among the Greeks and Italians, the god of the oak was also the god of rain and thunder, who carried great power for growth and regeneration.

Another example of tree worship is seen in the meaning of the ancient Teutonic word for "temple," which loosely translates as "woods." These ancient Germans considered trees sacred to the extent that the life of a man was taken for harming the life of a tree.

The Celts in ancient Briton and other parts of Europe are well-known for their veneration of trees. The oak groves in particular were sacred to the Celts. The philosophers, judges, and advisors of the tribal leaders were known as "Druids." The word "Druid" means "men of the oak trees." The Druid word for "sanctuary" seems to be identical with the Latin word "nemus" meaning "grove" or "woodland glade." From 600 B.C. to 700 A.D., the Druids communicated with each other by using a secret alphabet of twenty-five letters. Fourteen of the twenty-five letters were named after trees. The trees were chosen according to the way in which their natural qualities expressed spiritual concepts. Many historians have noted the similarities between the rituals of Dodona and those of the Druid priests of Britain and Gaul.

Trees were considered sacred in the New World as well as the Old World. The Hidatsa Indians honored the cottonwood for having the wisdom that could help the Indians with certain undertakings. Like the ancient Germans, they considered it wrong to fell a cottonwood, and only used trees that had fallen naturally. The Iroquois, as well as other Native American tribes, believed that each species of tree or plant had its own spirit, and that it was important to recognize and honor that spirit for its gift of service.

Ancient cultures that considered trees to be animate, also felt the pain of the tree being cut down. Some cultures asked for forgiveness when cutting a tree down, and others offered gifts to the trees.

TREES AS SYMBOLS OF REGENERATION AND RESURRECTION

History has shown us that trees have been treated as divine sources of wisdom, and worshipped as deities. They have also been recognized as symbols of regeneration and resurrection.

In ancient Egypt, Phoenicia, and Byblos, as well as in Christian legends, trees have been important symbols in myths about the sun. In the birth legend of the sun god Adonis, Smyrna, his mother, was turned into a myrrh tree by the gods. On December 24, a wild boar (which symbolizes winter) split the myrrh tree and Adonis was born.

In the Phrygian myth, Attis, the sun god, dies after emasculating himself under a pine tree, giving the tree immortality. After three days (months), on March 25, Attis arose from his tomb. This resurrection allowed him to overcome death for all who were initiated into his mysteries. This myth is considered by some to be the origin of the symbolism of the Christmas tree.

Another example of the tree as a symbol of regeneration and resurrection is the legend of the Tree of Life. Seth, the son of Adam and Eve, is sent on a mission to the Garden of Eden to retrieve the oil of mercy which God promised humankind. Instead he is given three seeds from the Tree of Life (some say the Tree of Knowledge). The tree from which he receives the seeds is in the shape of a cross. These seeds were placed in Adam's mouth when he died and grew into a sapling with three trunks in one, which Noah dug up and took with him on the ark. After the flood, Noah planted the tree on the summit of Mt. Lebanon. The legend relates how the wood of this holy tree eventually becomes the wood from which Jesus' cross was made.

It is possible that the tree Noah was to have taken with him on the ark also became known as "The Tree of Noah." This tree grew from the roof of the ark, and depicted the nations founded by Noah's three sons. Most Bibles of the Middle Ages devoted a section to these genealogical tables which showed the descent of humanity from

Adam and Eve to Jesus Christ. "The Tree of Noah" is most likely the origin of the genealogical "family tree."

In the New Testament, there is the miraculous tree of Revelation which bore twelve kinds of fruit and whose leaves were for the healing of the nations. These references all bear witness to the esteem in which trees where held by the scribes of the Holy Writ.

Trees as a symbol of regeneration and resurrection are prominent in the customs of various cultures. For example, in China, it is customary to plant a cypress or a pine on the grave of the deceased, in order to strengthen his or her soul and save the body from corruption.

Evergreen wreaths of laurel, olive, myrtle, or oak were used in the rituals in Greek, European, and Christian cultures to signify the perpetuity of youth and vigor, and therefore the continuation of existence.

Trees were often a part of ceremonies enacted in order to insure the growth of bountiful crops. In German and French tradition, for example, either a large branch or a whole tree was decked with ears of corn, brought home on the last wagon from the harvest field, and fastened to the roof of the farmhouse. It remained there for a year to bring about a fruitful corn harvest.

A variety of customs that we can loosely term "the maypole," were a part of spring and summer celebrations taking place from the thirteenth century onward. A tree was cut down every year (or sometimes the same tree was used for several years) and tree branches were fastened on every house, in order to bring the blessings of the tree spirit. The tree was decked with ribbons and set up, and the people of the village would dance around it.

Trees have nourished body, mind, and spirit for thousands of years and remain a source of wisdom, beauty, and inspiration.

4 | Branching Out— Modern Pioneers into the Spiritual Realm of Nature

THE PEOPLE DESCRIBED in this chapter have sought in different ways to explore the non-physical or spiritual dimension of Nature. *They all share a common perception that everything in Nature consists of life-force energy, vibrating at different frequencies.* On the physical level life-force energy ultimately becomes matter, and on the spiritual level, it is Consciousness, or the God in All Life. We may experience God or Consciousness as Joy, Peace or an all-encompassing Love. *The Higher Self* is the part of us that is connected with Consciousness, and which radiates Unconditional Love.

Everything created in Nature, every rock, tree, animal, or human therefore has a physical dimension and a spiritual dimension—a form and Consciousness. Physical form in Nature, then, is a Divine Expression of Consciousness. The terms *Nature Intelligences, Angels, Devas,* and *Nature Spirits* that are used in this chapter all refer to the Spiritual Consciousness of Nature, and God in All Life.

The existence of the non-physical dimension of the natural world and the role that this spiritual dimension can play in human health, is not well understood in modern Western culture. However there have been a small number of people who had a strong desire to explore the unknown areas of the mind and spirit as they relate to Nature.

PARACELSUS

Perhaps one of the better-known doctors, whose ideas were forerunners of health concepts that are relevant to our study, was Paracelsus (1490–1540). Paracelsus was known in his own day as "the Swiss Hermes," and he was deeply interested in the studies of both medicine and theology.

Paracelsus believed that true knowledge was attained through "intuition" and experience. The purpose of intuition was to reveal certain basic ideas which must then be observed and tested through experience. According to Paracelsus, intuition is possible because of the existence in Nature of a "universal life force," which he compared to light. There is light, the physical radiance that comes from a source such as a candle, and there is invisible light, which is the Cause of Wisdom. The outer light is like a physical representation of Inner Light.

Paracelsus' approach to learning was to observe the structure, form, color, and aroma of plants and other forms in Nature, and to let his observations lead him intuitively to their usefulness to humankind. He believed that the outer form was a guide to a plant's purpose in healing. After he had gathered his information, he would experiment practically, and he became well-known as a successful herbalist. Paracelsus promoted many ideas that were unorthodox for his time. Some of these ideas are currently accepted concepts in the field of holistic health. For example, he believed that overexertion and the excessive consumption of food and alcohol contributed to disease, and he therefore encouraged moderation in living. He also declared that many diseases originated in psychological causes. Above all, Paracelsus sought to restore health through natural means, in harmony with the simple truths of life.

Paracelsus also described the "Intelligence of Nature," based on his beliefs in an invisible world that is mirrored by the outer world. Paracelsus called the beings on the invisible planes *elementals* because they were composed of a single element. He believed that these elementals did not have a soul or a moral nature, so therefore they were more like animals. Following the concepts of Greece, Egypt, India, and China, Paracelsus divided the elemental beings into four groups: earth spirits or *gnomes*, water spirits or *nymphs*, fire spirits or *salamanders*, and air spirits or *sylphs*. He wrote that the elementals not only lived within their particular elements but were the administrators of the processes associated with these elements.

In other words, they were the "guiding intelligences" behind the "instinctive" knowledge of animals, as well as the formation of clouds, earthquakes, storms, etc. He gave them a number of human attributes in describing them as specific groups or races, ruled by kings and princes.

Our modern tales of fairies, giants, and gnomes who reveal their treasures to aware mortals have been influenced by the beliefs and writings of Paracelsus. Until relatively recently, our understanding of Nature beyond the physical realm has come largely through mythology, folklore, and symbolism.

RAOUL FRANCÉ

At the beginning of the twentieth century, a gifted Viennese biologist named Raoul Francé sought to describe plants in scientific terms as living beings with some sort of non-physical consciousness. He advanced the idea that plants were capable of movement, extraordinary perception, and communication. He felt that the current understanding of plants was limited, partly due to the time needed for observation.

First of all, he states that plants are capable of *intent*. They can stretch toward what they want and they appear to perceive and react to what is happening in their environment at a level of sophistication that is far greater than our own. The sundew plant, for example, will reach for a fly with infallible accuracy, moving directly toward its prey.

Secondly, Francé states that plants which react so certainly to the outer world, must have some means of communicating with the outer world, something superior to our five senses, because they are constantly observing and recording phenomena of which we know nothing. The ingenuity of plants in devising forms of construction far exceeds that of human engineers. A tree for example, grows upward and thickens just the right amount to support its greater height. We do not know how to pump liquid up to great heights as efficiently as trees do daily, to maintain themselves.

Because the external form of the plant is kept as a unit and restored whenever part of it is destroyed, Francé assumed that there must be some conscious entity supervising the entire form, some intelligence directing the plant either from within or without. He was one of the pioneer scientists who demonstrated that plants will react violently against abuse and will also give much gratitude for kind treatment.

Francé's ideas were considered shocking, and were largely ignored in his time. However, since the 1960s, his pioneering efforts have been confirmed by scientists who have begun to prove that plants do indeed have intent, and can communicate with humans. *The Secret Life of Plants* by Peter Tompkins and Christopher Bird details a number of fascinating experiments illustrating how plants communicate, and how they respond to the beliefs and attitudes of humans. It is our resistance to change that mires us in the ignorance of viewing plants as decorative, relatively inert "things" to be used in some way, rather than as living, communicating beings.

LUTHER BURBANK

Luther Burbank was another early twentieth century scientist who regarded plants as living beings with a spiritual consciousness. Burbank (1849–1926) became well-known as the "Wizard of Horticulture," for producing over 800 new strains and varieties of plants through hybridization. He created many new plants through selective breeding, cross-pollination, and grafting during a time when the predominant horticultural view considered it impossible to produce much variation in plants. He remained an enigma to orthodox scientists because of his belief that *"the secret of improved plant breeding, apart from scientific knowledge, is love* [italics added]."[1]

Burbank was born in 1849 in Lancaster, Massachusetts. During his education he was strongly influenced by the reverence for nature that he found in the works of Thoreau, and the naturalists Alexander von Humboldt and Louis Agassiz. Darwin's theory of evolution inspired him to create plants that served a purpose that would benefit humankind.

One of his first projects was the breeding of a new and larger white potato, which was received enthusiastically by growers in the San Joaquin Valley of California. Their acceptance of this potato, replacing the currently grown red-skinned potato, is now our most common variety called "the Burbank potato."

Burbank decided to move to Santa Rosa, California where he published his first catalogue in 1892. This fifty-two page catalogue entitled "New Creations in Fruits and Flowers" caused a considerable sensation in the horticultural world, where the development of new plants was unheard of. One listing was the well-known Shasta daisy. Another listing was the Paradox walnut tree, which could form a hedge tall enough in a few years to screen a house. With this same tree, he proved that natural evolution can be hastened. The tree produced walnuts after sixteen years, half the time that is normally required. Luther Burbank went on to write extensively about his work in two books that totaled twenty volumes, and continued his series of descriptive catalogues.

There was much controversy about his methods because he had no laboratory, kept few notes, and insisted that he had no "rational" explanation for his methodology. He described his art as "a matter of concentration" and the rapid elimination of non-essentials. He was considered a man of patience and enthusiasm, with a remarkably acute judgement of the merits and capabilities of plants. He could walk down a row of tiny seedlings and pick out almost instantaneously those most likely to succeed.

One person to whom Burbank was more specific about his methods was the philosopher and mystic, Manly P. Hall, founder of the Philosophical Research Society in Los Angeles. According to Hall, Burbank's power of love for his plants was the nourishment that made everything grow better and bear fruit more abundantly. When he wanted his plants to develop in a particular way not common to their kind, he would get down on his knees and take them into his confidence, ask them for help, and assure them that he held their lives in deepest respect and affection. Burbank was convinced that by some telepathy, they understood his meaning.

A well-known example of this approach was his development of spineless cacti, for the use of forage for livestock. He talked to the cacti, telling them that they had nothing to fear, and thereby would not need their defensive thorns. By creating a vibration of love and trust the plants gradually emerged thornless and became a new variety.

His philosophy is well-expressed in a lecture to the American Pomological Society:

> In pursuing the study of any of the universal and everlasting laws of nature, whether relating to the life, growth, structure, and movements of a giant planet, the tiniest plant or of psychological movements of the human brain, some conditions are necessary before we can become one of nature's interpreters or the creator of any valuable work for the world. Preconceived notions, dogmas, and all personal prejudice and bias must be laid aside. Listen patiently, quietly and reverently to the lessons,

one by one, which Mother Nature has to teach, shedding Light on that which was before a mystery, so that all who will, may see and know. She conveys her truths only to those who are passive and receptive. Accepting these truths as suggested, wherever they may lead them, we have the whole universe in harmony with us. At last man has found a solid foundation for science, having discovered that he is part of a universe which is eternally unstable in form, and eternally immutable in substance.[2]

He once stated to his friend, the yoga master Paramahansa Yogananda:

I see humanity now as one vast plant, needing for its highest fulfilments only love, the natural blessings of the great outdoors, and intelligent crossing and selection. In the span of my own lifetime I have observed such wondrous progress in plant evolution that I look forward optimistically to a healthy, happy world as soon as its children are taught the principles of simple and rational living. We must return to nature and nature's god.[3]

SEMYON AND VALENTINA KIRLIAN

Another non-physical dimension of plants that scientists have been studying is the "life-force energy field" that surrounds them. The Kirlians, a husband and wife team, have become well-known for their photographic work with these life-force energy fields. In 1950 Semyon and Valentina Kirlian were experimenting in Russia with a new technique of photographing a strange luminescence that seemed to come from all living things, but which was not visible to the human eye. A scientist who came to visit, asked them to photograph two leaves which were identical in appearance. The photographs, however, showed one leaf with a very strong luminescence and the other with a very weak luminescence. The scientist then told them that the leaf with the bright field was from a healthy plant, while the leaf with a dim field was from a diseased plant. The experiment proved that perceiving and studying the energy field of a plant revealed things about the plant that were not visible to the naked eye. This experience initiated the Kirlians into an extensive period of photographing these fields, for which they became known in the 1960s. They were also able to show photographically that a leaf with a piece torn out will still radiate the energy field of a whole leaf, illustrating that the energy field is an organizing pattern or template for the physical form. Here was another clue about how the "organizing intelligence" of plants works.

While scientists like Francé and the Kirlians have been moving in the direction of trying to prove the existence of the non-physical dimensions of plants, others have communicated with plants through their intuition or spiritual awareness, with the idea of co-creating something of benefit to others.

RICHARD ST. BARBE BAKER

Richard St. Barbe Baker, the "Man of the Trees," was estimated to have been directly or indirectly responsible for the planting and protection of over twenty-five billion trees. He was motivated by an intuitive sense of the unity of all living things. He expressed his deep love for trees as a pioneer of planetary ecology, a man of both vision and action. His dream was a world healed through the conservation of trees.

Baker was born in 1889, in Southampton, England, the son of a preacher and nurseryman. His early experiences as a farmer in Saskatchewan in 1910, and a lumberjack in England after being wounded in World War I, influenced his decision to study forestry at Cambridge University. He was very concerned about the trees that were being plowed under on the prairies and not replanted. He also decided that he would like to be in a position to speak out against the typical logging practices of clear-cutting. After graduation, he was posted to Kenya as the Assistant Conservator of Forests. To his dismay the role of conservator involved supervising the plunder of the African forest to fuel European industry, creating poorer soils, and hardship among the local people. He decided to enlist the help of the local chiefs in a reforestation project through a ritual dance to celebrate the spirit of the trees. This ceremony was attended by three thousand warriors, who promised before the High God to protect and plant trees each year. That was the beginning of *Men of the Trees*, which later became an international organization with affiliates in over one hundred countries.

Richard St. Barbe Baker traveled extensively, organizing local reforestation projects. He was even able to bring together hostile religious elements in Palestine to plant trees. In 1930 in America, he authored *Men of the Trees*, the first of thirty books. He was a vocal advocate of saving the redwoods in California, which became a fifty-year struggle. Other major contributions to American conservation were the reforestation projects that he proposed for the Civilian Conservation Corps, an effort of Franklin Roosevelt to employ people as well as to save the soil.

Perhaps Richard St. Barbe Baker began his most ambitious project in 1952 with the Sahara Reclamation Program. This program involved reclaiming two million square miles of the Sahara Desert, an area larger than Australia, by planting trees. At this time only several countries have attempted participation in this plan.

China has been a very active supporter of reforestation. In their efforts to hold back the desert, tree cover has been increased from seven to twenty-eight percent. Six hundred million Chinese have pledged to plant five trees annually—a planting of three billion trees a year.

Perhaps Richard St. Barbe Baker is not better-known because his philosophy did not support the damaging practices of big industry. He opposed clear-cutting and supported the selective cutting of trees, and their replacement through replanting. He advocated a garden system that emphasized poly-culture, tree farming, and human scale technology. He also believed that no semi-arid region can withstand long-term intensive tillage without the protection of trees. Baker recommended that one-third of every watershed be devoted to trees. He was also well-known for encouraging people, especially children, to hug trees. He describes a special tree from his childhood in the following manner:

> When I was feeling unhappy, or if things had gone wrong for me during the day, I would leave the house, run down the little lane, cross the meadow and visit a particular beech tree in the wood. That beech with smooth bark was a Mother Confessor to me—my Madonna of the Woods. Standing by the friendly beech, I knew in my heart that my troubles and my grief, as well as all that pleased me, were but for a passing moment. I would imagine that I had roots digging down deep into Mother Earth and that all above I was sprouting branches. I would hold that in my thoughts for a few moments and then come back with the strength of the tree and a radiant heart, knowing that that was all that really mattered.[4]

Four days before his death in 1981, he attended his last tree planting on June 5, World Environment Day. Around a freshly-planted poplar he led children in the motto of the *Children of the Green Earth*: "From our hearts, with our hands, for the earth, all the world together." These words describe the philosophy and spirit by which he lived.

DR. EDWARD BACH AND THE FLOWER REMEDIES

Dr. Edward Bach (1886–1936) was influenced by Paracelsus' ideas that health could be restored through means that were in harmony with Nature. He was perhaps the first modern "holistic" healer to teach others about the spiritual healing qualities of living plants. Bach was born on September 24, 1886 in England, the eldest of three children. Perhaps his favorite pastime as a boy was tramping in the mountains of Wales, where he spent a number of days and nights. Any human being or animal in pain aroused much compassion in him, and he was determined to be a doctor.

He practiced medicine in London from 1914 to 1930 and during the latter part of that time, he became well-known as a bacteriologist. His ideal was to find a simple way to cure all disease, and his first step in that direction was to develop a vaccine from intestinal bacteria that seemed to cleanse the system of poisons causing chronic disease.

One event early in his medical career was to have a profound effect on him. In 1917 he suffered a severe brain hemorrhage and was told that he had only three months to live. He continued with the work that he loved, which was the research on the vaccines, and made a full recovery, much to the surprise of his doctors. His own personal conclusion was that having a definite purpose in life is a deciding factor in regaining and remaining in good health.

In 1919 he accepted a post in bacteriology in a homeopathic hospital in London, and the ideas of Hahnemann stimulated him greatly. Hahnemann taught that healing commenced with the activation and enhancement of the "vital force." Hahnemann also used plant remedies from Nature, and he believed that the doctor must treat the patient and not the disease. Hahnemann was guided by the mental characteristics of the patient to the appropriate remedy. During this time Bach continued the development of his oral vaccines and also the careful observance of his patients' temperaments and personality characteristics.

Even though Bach's oral vaccines were successful, he wished to find purer remedies and determined that this would be the direction of his future research. He wanted to find living plants, because he felt that they were given to humankind by the Divine Creator for the purpose of bringing peace and harmony to the whole personality.

So in 1930, when he was forty-three years old, he decided to devote more time to his new direction in research. He divided up his extensive medical practice, closed down his laboratory, burned all his papers, and followed "a strong impulse" to return to Wales. He had no specific plans, only a "knowing" that he would find the healing methods that he was seeking. He spent many days walking in the hills and meadows, and came to the conclusion that he would use the flowerheads alone, for he felt that the life of the plant was concentrated in the flower. One morning in May it flashed through his mind that the dew on the plants must contain some of the properties of the plant, for the heat of the sun would serve to draw them out. This dew indeed turned out to be a potent remedy. To simplify the process, he decided to pick a few flowers and place them in a glass bowl. He filled the bowl with water from a clear stream and left it standing in the field in full sunlight for several hours. From then on, until 1936, he proceeded to create thirty-eight flower remedies in this manner, seventeen of which were from tree flowers.[5]

In his first book, *Heal Thyself*, published in 1933, he clearly states his belief that disease is not due to physical causes but to disturbed states of mind that interfere with happiness. In publishing his pamphlet *The Twelve Healers* in 1934, his goal was to encourage the public to heal themselves with the remedies.

Bach believed that the flower remedies alone could cure disease, and he acted with great courage and faith on those beliefs. He used nothing but the remedies to effect many cures of both chronic and acute illness, and was much in demand as a physician. Dr. Edward Bach died in his sleep at the age of fifty, having accomplished his goal of developing a healing system that cured disease and elevated human Divinity with the healing powers of Nature.

THE FINDHORN GARDEN

The Findhorn garden and cooperative community is considered by many to be a teaching model for cooperating with Nature, and for building communities that honor both individual needs and group needs. Findhorn was founded and developed by three people who were committed to their own spiritual growth, and to bringing beauty and peace to the Planet. Following their inner guidance, Peter and Eileen Caddy with their three children and their friend Dorothy MacLean, moved to Findhorn Caravan Park. They settled into this park in northern Scotland during a dark November day in 1962. They had no idea why they were led to go there, although they thought that the coming winter would be a time of spiritual retreat and purification before they would again seek employment in the spring.

The land at Findhorn was sandy and gravelly, often swept by gale force winds, and covered mainly with tough, pointed grass. Peter spent the winter reading gardening books for the garden they hoped to start in the spring, and Dorothy and Eileen meditated a great deal. Early spring found Peter digging up the ground, according to instructions given through Eileen's guidance. In May, Dorothy received in meditation that she was to communicate with the Spirits of the physical forms of the plants. Overwhelmed, she felt that she could not do this, but was encouraged by both Peter and Eileen. Dorothy chose to receive her first instructions from the garden pea, because she knew the plant well and she loved eating peas. She then focused on the Inner Essence or Spirit of the plant and received a communication, much to her surprise and wonderment. After that, Peter would give her a list of questions and she would address the appropriate plant. The work of the garden had begun.

The garden was an astonishing success, and it became obvious to the Caddys and Dorothy MacLean that they were involved in a revolutionary process that was to be a prototype of the new ways that humans could learn to relate to Nature. That first season their cabbages and brussels sprouts were the only ones in the country to survive a plague of cabbage root grubs. By May of 1964 they were growing thirty-pound cabbages and the county horticultural advisor was quite perplexed to find that there were no soil deficiencies in this organic garden. After several years word began to get around about this miracle garden, and many accomplished gardeners and agricultural experts visisted and were amazed at the quality of the plant life.

Meanwhile Dorothy MacLean had been developing her skills and was receiving much information from her communications with the plants. She learned that some were especially helpful for physical health, and others were especially good for healing the emotions. The plants helped her understand that human emotions affect plants. Negative emotions have a depressing effect on plants, while uplifting emotions have a beneficial effect, and the plants grow better. Dorothy also learned that she was addressing not the individual plant, but the "Overlighting Being" of the species. She called these Overlighting Beings "Devas," which is a Sanskrit term meaning "Shining Ones." Another being whom she contacted was the "Landscape Angel," an Overlighting Being for a geographical area who told her how to build compost to fortify the soil, and where to find the ingredients, since they did not have spare cash. The garden later became the center around which a community was built, for people to learn how to cooperate better among themselves, as well as with Nature.

Those involved with the Findhorn garden learned to see the soil, each plant, and each person as a unique entity with a specific purpose in building a harmonious, healthy environment for all— human and non-human. The quality of this environment was created through each individual's trust in their own intuitive guidance, the focusing of positive thoughts toward each other and toward the gardening process, and being receptive to the spiritual guidance of the Devas of the plants.

PERELANDRA

Inspired by the Findhorn garden books, Machaelle Small Wright declared her intent in the woods in January 1977, to learn from the Devas and Nature Spirits, and to establish a Nature research center. She began receiving information from the Devas and Nature Spirits, and committed herself to the process of building her garden. The Perelandra garden is a beautiful, one-hundred-foot circular garden, located in the foothills of the Blue Ridge Mountains in Virginia. Machaelle has developed what she calls "co-creative energy gardening," which emphasizes the balance of life force energy, and teamwork with the Nature Intelligences. Her garden is an environment that welcomes all animals and insects, rather than repelling or killing them.

In her books she clearly defines the difference between the Devas and the Nature Spirits: "Devas can be described as the intelligent level of consciousness within Nature that functions in an architectural mode within all that is of form, and also serves as the organizer of all that is a part of each form."[6] The term "Nature Spirit" refers to "the intelligent level of consciousness within Nature that works in partnership with the devic level and is responsible for the fusing and maintaining of energy to appropriate form."[7] For example, Machaelle Small Wright states that if you want to know something about the qualities of a plant, you would contact the Deva of that plant. If you want to know how much water to give it, you would contact the Nature Spirits that work with the plant.

In her books she describes how her garden progressed according to the guidance of the Devas and the Nature Spirits. She gives very clear directions on how to go about establishing contact with them, and how to ask the appropriate gardening questions. Wright has demonstrated in very concrete terms, how we may set about communicating with the Nature Intelligences and encourages us to get to work.

5 | Beginning Your Journey into the Magical World of Trees

OUR PERSONAL JOURNEY

Wʜᴇɴ I ᴡᴀs a child we lived in a suburban home surrounded by a few small, planted trees. However, we vacationed in Vermont, where I looked forward to being lulled to sleep by the wind in the pines. Although I took the trees for granted, I loved walking in the woods. Because it was summer, the trees spoke to me of freedom and new places to explore.

When Jonathan and I met in Pennsylvania in 1981, we discovered that we had a mutual interest in walking and hiking in the woods. This has not only become a major form of recreation for us, but has also provided a sanctuary in time of need. Over the years we have found ourselves retreating frequently to the woods for solace, in order to deal with issues of loneliness, illness and fear.

We remember a time in 1983 in one of our special places where I asked Jonathan, "Is there anything Nature wishes to share with us?" Jonathan became very still and asked for guidance and understanding to come through him. Usually the guidance that comes through his Higher Self is a presence of Unconditional Love that is of a personal and intimate nature. At this particular time, Jonathan experienced this guidance differently, as a more impersonal, all-encompassing Unconditional Love. The guidance itself was very helpful for the issues with which we were dealing at the time. But we knew that this was a new energy, which we defined as an energy of Nature since that is what we asked for. We learned that this particular guidance came from an Overlighting Deva for the geographical area where we were located. We then were even more determined to learn how to communicate with the Devas and the Nature Spirits, and it gradually became clear to us that the way to do this was through the stones and the trees. Thus, our own journey involved turning to the forces of Nature for healing.

We wish to add our own experiences to those of all the others who have said that it is time for Humankind to learn to work with Nature for personal and planetary healing. Once you get over the hurdle of thinking that it is unusual to communicate with trees, perhaps you will feel the suffering that we have felt expressed from the trees about being misunderstood. Our own connection with Nature has developed out of what we have needed to learn and what we love to do best. As you declare your intent and your willingness to work with Nature, your own way of connecting will open up for you also.

GETTING STARTED: ATTUNING YOURSELF WITH NATURE

We will suggest some steps that we have followed as a way of getting started with your own process. The first step is to *go to a natural woods*. Our guidance is that although every tree has spiritual qualities, those that are planted by humans serve a different purpose than those that are naturally growing in a forest. Particularly when you are beginning this process, it can be valuable to be where Nature is in her most balanced state. Allow yourself the flexibility of time to slow your rhythms, so that you can be more in harmony with Nature's rhythms.

The second step involves *relaxing your body and clearing your mind*, so that you can receive more insight. The physical exercise of walking will help you release worries and tension, so it is a good idea to walk for a while before trying to do anything else. As you begin walking, enjoy the woods with all of your senses. When you keep your attention focused on the little surprises around you, you may notice your mind relaxing, because the constant focus on the present becomes a walking meditation.

The third step is to *affirm your relationship with Nature*. Walk with a sense of *gratitude* for everything you see, for the Love present everywhere. Trees and plants register life-force energy to a greater degree than we can, and thus they perceive and store much information about the energy fields with which they come in contact. Therefore they are sensitive to your energies and they pick up on your Unconditional Love for them. The Overlighting Deva for the Plant Kingdom comments on attitude:

> Enter our domain with an open accepting, pure heart. There is much that we can share with you about ways of understanding the complexities of living in a physical vehicle. Come without expectations and be curious and sensitive as a child is. Then you will be ready to receive us.

You have shared your love and gratitude with the trees, and now you are ready for the fourth step, which is *to allow yourself to be attracted to one particular tree.* This tree will most likely be one whose qualities you need at the moment, so let your intuition guide you.

It is important to ask permission to work with the tree for two main reasons. One is that some trees have had damaging contacts with humans somewhere in their growth cycle, and they may not wish to be of service to you in the way that you would like. The second reason is that especially during the fall or winter, a dormant tree may wish to preserve its life-force energy for the coming growth cycle. This can be true for older trees that have been weakened in some manner, or trees that are under stress in their particular locations. You cannot tell just by looking at a tree whether or not it would enjoy giving to you.

Jonathan and I have both had the experience of trees reaching out to us when we were especially needy, but then at a later time indicating that they did not want to teach us on a regular basis. If you feel strongly attracted to a tree, it wishes to be of service to you. Before you start feeling guilty about possibly hurting a tree, remember that the tree understands that you are in a learning process. Take the step and ask permission to be with the tree, and ask for a particular sign that says, "No, I wish not to be with you at this time." You will be indicating by your intent and your commitment that you are willing to learn.

The fifth step is to *deepen you meditative or "spiritually aware" state.* When you are in Nature, this is when you are experiencing the majesty of a sunset, or a place where beauty is an experience beyond words. The superlative, timeless quality of the joy of being alive is a spiritual connection with Nature. Affirm your Oneness with the tree, and your Oneness with All of Life, honoring the tree and opening to its wisdom. We will give some further suggestions for deepening your spiritual attunement with a tree later in this chapter.

The sixth step when asking for guidance from a tree is to *open to the energy field of the tree.* When you walk in the woods, one of the reasons if feels so peaceful, is that you have entered an area of interconnecting energy fields that is balanced. Your Higher Self, or the part of you that is connected to All That Is, often perceives these energy fields in terms of spiritual qualities such as peace, joy and beauty.

In the same way that some of you have learned to sense the energy fields of stones by holding them and asking the God Within You to help you sense the God Within the Stone, you can also learn to sense the life-force energy field of a tree.

Jonathan and I often lean against a tree with our backs to the trunk. You can also hug the tree, for they enjoy this expression of appreciation. When your whole body is in physical contact with the tree, you can receive an "energy balancing." This is also what happens when you hold a stone. You may feel a surge of energy inside your body, and when it tapers off and your energy becomes still, the balancing is complete. In our experience, the whole process takes only a few minutes. It doesn't matter whether or not you can sense the process, because it takes place anyway. The important thing is to give yourself time in physical contact with the tree, and allow yourself to receive Love. It is like receiving a treatment from anyone who works with an energy system such as crystal balancing, reiki, therapeutic touch, or polarity. This is, however, a do-it-yourself energy treatment. You will find your experience with the tree both rejuvenating and relaxing. Your energy is also balanced when you are standing near a tree or walking in the woods, but it is a gentler process and generally takes a lot longer.

The seventh step after your energy is balanced is to *ask the tree Deva for the guidance that you need.* You can ask a more general question such as, "Can you help me understand how to bring more balance into my life?" Or, you can ask specific questions such as, "How do I need to love myself in order to heal physically?" or "What is my next step on my spiritual path?"

If you wish to work with the tree qualities like those that are given in Part Two, you can ask, "What qualities of your being do I need to affirm?" A tree Deva (or a stone or animal Deva) can share from a broad spiritual perspective, and so it is possible to receive a different answer for each of the above questions. *Your intent* or *the level of understanding that you seek* determines how you perceive the response. Here are some comments from the Grand Fir Deva on what creates an effective flow of communication between the Human Kingdom and the Devic Kingdom:

> First, you need to view the tree species as a parallel reality that is neither greater nor less than you are. You then need to release any expectations surrounding the particular process with a tree. In other words, be open and receptive to the exchange that takes place in whatever form in which you receive it. When you first begin the process, it may seem like nothing is happening to you. This is not a sign for you to throw your hands into the air and decide that it is not worth it. There must be patience so that the flow itself can develop fully. It is a process of letting down the language barriers between you and the tree species.
>
> When you enter the domain of the trees it must be done without a time pressure. You must honor their particular flow and synchronize their flow with yours. Give yourself whatever space is needed for the process involved. My words can be summed up in encouraging you to release all judgment from the process.

The final step is that once you have asked a tree to share its energy with you, it is important for you to *thank the tree by giving it your Unconditional Love.* One way that Jonathan and I do this is by affirming three or four times, "I give you my Love, for your growth and the fulfillment of your purpose." This is a wonderful experience of Oneness, and is a learning in itself. The tree will take in your energy, and may let you know when the interaction is complete. For example, you may "have a thought" that it is all right to leave the area.

We could summarize these eight steps for communicating with the trees in the following manner:

1. Walk in a natural area, if possible.
2. Relax your body and clear your mind.
3. Affirm Love and Gratitude for Nature.

4. Allow yourself to be attracted to a tree, and ask for permission to work with it.
5. Deepen your spiritual connection with the tree.
6. Balance your energies through physical contact with the tree.
7. Ask for the guidance that you seek.
8. Thank the tree for its help and energy.

DEEPENING YOUR ATTUNEMENT WITH A TREE

At this point we would like to return to step five, and comment further on deepening your attunement with a tree. One way that you can bring yourself into a deeper spiritual place with a tree is to slow down your breathing, with gentle, deep breaths. Then allow your breath to go where it wants to go, and affirm that you are breathing with the tree. . . . Continue to breathe and become one with the tree. . . . This process does not need to take more than a few minutes.

You can also work with the following meditation for becoming one with the tree:

> I welcome you into my presence. . . . Let me share with you my being. . . . We begin under the ground with my roots. . . . Feel each tiny root as it reaches out through the soil for water and minerals. . . . Feel the anchoring that my roots give to me. . . . Allow your awareness to be with my trunk, the central structure of my being. . . . As nourishment travels up my trunk, be aware of all the cells that sustain my growth. . . . Let the bigness and stability of my trunk enfold and support you. . . . As your awareness travels through my branches, enjoy the patterns that they make against the sky. . . . Visit with my leaves, as they catch the sunlight and the air to make new food for me. . . . See the lovely green that I create for you with the sunbeams. . . . Be aware of the unique specialness of each leaf. . . . Let it be spring in your mind, and watch my flowers bud and bloom, and let the wind blow them away to make new life. . . . Enjoy my quiet endurance, and know that you are Home, here with me. . . .

We found it helpful, particularly in the beginning, to carry with us a clear quartz crystal, programmed to aid with Devic communication. To do this, you can mentally affirm that you wish to deepen your attunement with the Devas, and then you focus into the crystal your sense of total connectedness with Nature. For further information on programming crystals, see chapter five in *The Newcastle Guide to Healing With Crystals.*

We have suggested some ways that you can deepen your spiritual awareness in preparation for the seventh step of communicating with a particular tree Deva. It can be helpful to know that you have a choice in which level of Deva to address. Machaelle Small Wright describes a Deva as an architect of the physical form. We can also think of a Deva as the *Higher Self* of the physical form, or the *Consciousness of the form that is connected with All of Life.* It is important to understand that there is a hierarchy of Devas who operate with varying amounts of responsibility.

The Deva for each individual tree has a greater awareness of the needs of a particular tree in a given moment, because its unique pattern is always present before it. This Deva is like the contractor who directly oversees the work being done in the creation of the particular tree.

The Deva for a tree species is like a master planner for the evolution of that species, and can give a broader spectrum of qualities that the family has for working with the Human Kingdom.

The Deva for a geographical area oversees the pattern of growth for a number of species. For example, when there has been a disruption of the life-force energies in a given regional area, the Deva is immediately aware of the circumstances and communicates what is needed for balance in the region, to the Devas at other levels. This is the kind of Deva that Dorothy MacLean called "The Landscape Angel." An Overlighting Deva for an area can give a more comprehensive understanding about the human growth process, as well as the natural growth process, and the balance in a given geographic region.

You can choose to ask for guidance from a particular Deva, according to the kind of information that you wish to receive. If you want information on a specific health problem, you could choose any level of Deva. If you wish to know about an individual tree's perspective on life based on its own growth history, you would contact the individual tree Deva. Most of our work has been done with the species Devas because we have been interested in the spiritual qualities and guidance from the larger perspective of the species. If you are walking in the woods and wish to ask for help and guidance in being more at peace, then you would communicate with the Over-lighting Deva for a geographic region.

At this point trying to choose the appropriate Deva may seem a little overwhelming, but do not worry. In our experience, what actually happens is that your concerns are referred to the Deva that can provide you the level of understanding for which you are asking. Part of the reason that we discuss the different Devas is because we wish to stress the importance of your *intent* and your *perceptions*. You or other people can receive very different kinds of information from the same tree, depending on how you focus your concerns, and how you perceive your relationship with the tree.

While you are in the woods, an exercise you might try in order to further understand your own perception of Devic energy is as follows:

> Breathe yourself into a quiet space, and affirm the presence of your Higher Self. . . . Allow yourself to receive Unconditional Love and Peace from your Higher Self, to feel totally connected to All That Is. . . . Now affirm the presence of a particular tree Deva, as you become One with the tree. . . . Give yourself time to be receptive. . . . Once again, be aware of the difference in how you perceive this energy. . . . You can repeat the process for further observation.

You can also try working with a pendulum, asking, "Am I now connected with my Higher Self?" and then, "Am I now connected with the Deva?" and learning from the feedback that you receive. In using the pendulum you have the advantage of being able to ask questions such as, "Do I need to relax more?" or "Do I need to focus more on Unconditionally Loving this tree?" For more information on working with pendulums, see chapter four in *The Newcastle Guide to Healing With Crystals*.

If you don't notice any differences between your Higher Self and a Devic energy, just proceed on with your commitment to connect with Nature, and try the exercise another time.

It can be difficult to tell the differences between Higher Self energy and Devic energy, but if you perceive visually, the patterns of color and light may change. For Jonathan, the energy is more impersonal and all-encompassing. Remember, the way in which you receive spiritual perceptions is unique to you, and it is important to trust your own intuitive process.

Your beliefs about spiritual consciousness affect how you perceive Devic energy. Some people have named the various Devas, or given names to their favorite trees, as a way of affirming that the trees are living beings. Devas and Nature Spirits have the ability to take on a physical form, in order to help those who are learning to deepen their spiritual connection by perceiving them in this manner. This is why some people have seen fairies, elves and other physical forms. I also believe that those who perceive the spiritual dimensions in a visual manner are more likely to perceive visual forms. Children, and those adults who are able to retain childlike qualities, have also been more likely to see fairies, because this form can communicate the beauty, innocence and joyfulness of Devic energy.

I used to think that perhaps I was not perceiving Devic energy because I had not seen fairies. Now I realize that the manner in which we perceive is highly individual, and all that matters is the purity of the connection and how we act upon it.

Your beliefs will also influence the kind of information that you receive from a tree. If, for example, you believe that all trees are essentially feminine in nature, then the information you receive will reflect that belief. It follows then, that our perceptions are going to reflect our personal beliefs and ways of perceiving. So work with our material according to your own understandings.

As the Grand Fir Deva stated earlier, this process of learning to communicate with the trees takes time and patience. For us it has been years of fine-tuning the experiences that we have always felt in the woods. The trees, through the Grand Fir Deva, want us all to know that:

> Any time that you extend love and nurturance to any life form on the planet, that love becomes an aspect of healing for Mother Earth. Visualize the Unconditional Love that you give to a tree, going to all other members of the species, to the whole forest, and to the entire Planet. Then all of life can benefit from your exchange of love with the tree, and you will be making a significant contribution to the wellbeing of the Earth on which we live.

Children have the capacity for a very special connection with Nature. We share the following story of seven-year-old Jennifer and her bad dream, not only with children of all ages, but with those adults who are in touch with their own "inner child." It is interesting to note that in the native cultures of the Philippines, people are encouraged to talk to trees when they have had bad dreams. This story is written by Pamela and illustrated by Aymalee, a dear friend who also works with Devic energy.

6 | Jennifer and the Little Fir

SEVEN-YEAR-OLD Jennifer woke up early that morning feeling unhappy, and she tried to snuggle deeper under the covers. In the darkness, the hurtful memories drifted back. She was still angry at her brother Tommy because yesterday he tried to take away her prized possession—a special wooden Kachina doll that her father had given her. Tommy had laughed when he made her cry.

And last night she had had a dream where some men with yellow hair, and strange helmets with horns on them, had attacked the farm where she was living. In the dream she wore very different clothes, and from a hiding place in the bushes she watched the men burn the small wooden buildings. Then they took her favorite thing—a beautiful wooden chest. . . . As she lay there remembering her dream she realized that she did not feel very good. Her tummy hurt, and she still felt angry and frightened.

Jennifer's mother called her for breakfast, and Jennifer stumbled into her overalls and a blouse, and wandered into the kitchen. This morning her favorite cereal reminded her of paste. Jennifer's mother was busy getting the trash ready to go out, and Jennifer could smell the soup for lunch, already bubbling on the stove. "Mommy, I don't fell very good," said Jennifer with a lump in her throat. It seemed like it would feel good to talk to someone.

"Why don't you run outside and play and I'm sure you will feel better," replied her mother, as she stirred the soup with one hand

and wiped the kitchen counter with the other. "I am trying to get the kitchen cleaned before my meeting." Jennifer sighed. Sometimes she wished her mother wouldn't keep herself so busy.

Jennifer tried to find her Daddy, who was shaving in the bathroom. "Daddy, I had a dream last night."

"Well, maybe you can tell me about it this evening, I have to get ready for work." Jennifer silently watched her father hurrying to wash the shaving cream off his face, and wished that there was someone here to listen to her now.

Feeling a little lonely, Jennifer walked outside and decided to go into the woods to the secret rock. The dark shade of the evergreens felt cool and soothing and just right. She stooped down to say hello to Solomon the Mushroom, to see if he had any frog visitors. He didn't. She gently lifted a rotten log next to Solomon, and there was a small, olive-colored salamander, still sleeping. The salamander

didn't seem to want to be bothered either. She gently replaced the log, and sat down to make a hill house of the little grown needles that were everywhere. They smelled good when she crumbled them in her hands.

Suddenly she heard a high, piping voice. "Jennifer, Jennifer, over here!" She looked around and nobody was there. "Jennifer, Jennifer, it's me, your new friend!" Jennifer looked carefully all around, but nobody was there. All she really noticed was a little fir tree off to the right. "Jennifer, Jennifer, come talk to me!"

Why, was that a little smiling face on the bark? Curiously, Jennifer walked toward the little fir. Its needles began quivering and she thought it might just jump out of its roots! "Oh Jennifer, I've been waiting such a long time for you to notice me!" Suddenly Jennifer felt tender arms giving her a big hug.

"Have you been talking to me?" Jennifer asked.

"Of course. I talk to you every time you visit Solomon Mushroom, but this is the first time that you have heard me. Oh, I am so happy!" The tree's branches quivered again. "Come closer so I can see you better. My, you are as beautiful as I thought you were, all sparkly with gold lights."

"Oh," cried Jennifer. She didn't know what else to say.

"See my new needles?" The fir quivered again and she suddenly noticed the new green needles at the tip of a low branch. How soft and bright they were! Then she felt the big hug again.

"How can you hug me when you don't have any arms?" she asked.

"Oh, it's easy," said the fir. "Just hug me now and you'll see."

Jennifer put her arms around the fir, which was not difficult since the tree was kind of thin, after all. Jennifer's cheek rested against the cool bark, which was just a little scratchy. Slowly she felt just like she did when her mother or her daddy hugged her—all snuggly on the inside and warm on the outside.

"Why, that feels wonderful," she said.

"I am full of surprises, you see, and I know lots of things too," said the little fir excitedly. "Will you be my friend and play with me?"

"Of course I will," said Jennifer. She felt a little shy with being showered with all this kindness from her new friend.

"Could you stroke me just here, my bark itches," the little fir pleaded. Jennifer felt like putting her hand on a certain spot on the bark, and she pretended that the tree was her little kitten.

"Ah, that feels much better," the little fir said, "Now we can play with this little breeze." Jennifer felt a soft puff of air on her face. And then she watched, the needles on one branch shook, and then the whole branch bobbed up and down. "That breeze tickles me so hard that I can hardly stop laughing," wheezed the fir. Jennifer smiled. She listened to the breeze playing with the little fir's needles, until the breeze gave her face a final caress, and was gone.

"Tell me about yourself. You looked a little sad, in fact, when I first saw you." At that, Jennifer felt the tears gathering behind her eyes and suddenly they fell like rain, and she leaned up against the little fir, sobbing.

"Tommy grabbed my doll away from me yesterday and laughed and I was so mad," Jennifer cried, "And I had a terrible dream last night."

"Tell me about your dream," said the little fir very gently.

"I, I dreamed that I lived on a farm and these big men with yellow hair and helmets burned my house and took my special wooden chest." The tears in Jennifer's throat caught the words and made them hard to say.

"Jennifer, you just relax right up against me, like that. I can see it was a very scary dream." The little fir held her very close, and Jennifer began to feel a little sleepy. Soon she was dreaming again . . .

This time she saw a beautiful angel with a rainbow halo, coming toward her. The angel looked at her with much love, took her hand, and said, "Come with me."

They went to the top of a hill, where Jennifer could see many mountains and valleys far, far away. The sky was pink and gold and lavender because the sun was setting. The angel pointed to the nearest valley, and Jennifer could see the farm of her earlier dream. The buildings were burning, and there was a little girl hidden in some brush. She was crying. The angel said, "Put your arms around that girl, and tell her how much you love her."

The fir tree appeared near the angel, and Jennifer suddenly felt herself holding the little girl and telling her, "It's all right, I am right here and I love you." This young girl seemed strangely familiar to Jennifer and then in a flash Jennifer understood. "Why, that's me," she thought. And that farm was where I lived a long, long time ago. Now she understood why she had been so frightened.

Just then, she saw her brother Tommy who now had yellow hair, climbing the hill toward her. She remembered that he was one of the men who had burned the farm. He was carrying a large,

wooden chest. "Oh, my beautiful wooden chest, you have brought it back," she cried.

Tommy hung his head and said, "I'm sorry I took your chest and everything else. Will you forgive me?" Then he disappeared.

"What a strange thing for Tommy to say," thought Jennifer, but somehow it didn't seem strange at all.

Jennifer and the little girl who was also herself opened the chest. Inside was the wooden Kachina doll and all sorts of other treasures. As the two girls reached inside to take out the treasures, the wooden chest disappeared.

The angel then said, "Remember that your treasures are already in your heart, and that you can always call upon me to help remember your treasures." With that, the angel took the hand of the little girl that was herself, and together they melted into a ball of light . . .

Jennifer rubbed her eyes and sat up, and found a sunbeam staring her right in the face. "Are you feeling better now?" asked the little fir.

"Oh, yes!" breathed Jennifer. "What a wonderful dream, I. . . ." And then she stopped because somehow she knew that the little fir had been right there with her. "Thank you, little fir. You found me when I needed you." Jennifer realized that her tummy felt fine and she began to think of all her favorite places in the woods that she had yet to visit today.

The little fir's branches quivered. "I hope that you will come to visit me again very soon. You are such a beautiful little girl." Jennifer threw her arms around the little fir and held the tree tightly.

"You are my dear, dear friend, and I love you very much." She heard a sigh, and felt the soft brush of angel wings on her back. Gently she patted the little fir's bark, and said, "Good-bye, little fir." As she made her way through the ferns, she looked back, and the little fir stood in the light of the sun, with sun sparkles dancing off its needles. "I have made a very special friend indeed," she thought.

7 | Under the Bodhi Tree: Trees as Spiritual Teachers

WHY COMMUNICATE WITH TREES?

THIS IS A TIME of spiritual awakening for Humankind. We are learning to see our life experiences as promoting the growth of our souls. We are also learning that we must choose of our own free will to be connected to God/Goddess/All That Is. The grand Fir Deva speaks about our spiritual purpose in learning to communicate with the trees:

> From my perspective, many within the Human Kingdom continue to live within a vacuum where they see themselves as elevated above other forms of life on the planet, and thus separate from them. You are coming to a personal awareness that you have a far deeper connection with other forms of life than you have realized.
>
> Trees, and in truth all the Kingdoms of Nature, take on a physical form in order to give service to Humankind in your soul evolution. For it is true for us as it is true for you: the more that you teach something of spiritual value, the more the evolution of your being is accelerated. So we learn through our service to you.

55

Every physical form in Nature radiates a spiritual essence that reflects both an individuality and a Oneness With All Of Life. You can learn from us that you truly can maintain an individual sense of self, while remaining connected with your Spiritual Source.

You can also learn from us what it means to give and receive Unconditional Love. By loving yourself unconditionally you come to see yourself as an aspect of the Divine, and you will know that you are always in connection with the Divine Source. In truth, the more that you access your spiritual dimension, the less imbalance you will have within your physical vehicle, and the more peace you will feel inside on an ongoing basis.

As you accept us as spiritual teachers, you will learn that there is no such thing as separateness in your Human Kingdom as well. There is only Oneness. We can help you see your own journey from a broader perspective, and you will find yourself less resistant to change and more open to the goodness and beauty that is all around you.

THE AGE OF A TREE

As you honor your own spiritual nature and begin to communicate with trees as spiritual teachers, a whole new world opens up to you. One of our first experiences was learning that the age of a tree is in itself a teaching. We first discovered this by attuning to the species qualities of a very large and old Douglas fir. We were surprised to find a considerable lack of species qualities. It seemed to us, instead, that this old Fir had somehow accomplished its purpose as an individual tree, and had reached a sense of completeness or Oneness with the Source. Intrigued, we decided to study a very young tree. Jonathan was drawn to a young Western hemlock in our neighborhood. We felt a strong sense of aliveness from this tree. Its energy turned out to be exuberant and energetic, like the energy of a puppy dog.

We went back to the elder Douglas fir and Jonathan asked the Deva to tell us about what can be learned from the age of a tree:

When a tree is at the beginning stages of its physical life cycle, there is a very strong energy connection with the earth itself. From a purely physical standpoint, a tree's survival depends on the strength of this connection. So from a young tree you can learn the importance of connecting with the physical earth plane. Young trees are the most energizing for the physical body.

A young tree is emerging in its growth cycle, and developing a vibrant and expanding sense of self. It says very clearly, ''It's great to be alive!'' When you have doubts about who you are and make the choice to affirm that it is good to be alive, you will have a greater sense of purpose and meaning in your life. You will find that the answers about who you are will come with greater clarity. A young tree can also teach you about how to be more open to your creative self, and how to live life more joyously.

As a tree grows in size and develops deeper roots, there is a transformation in its energy where its focus is not as much on survival. Rather, the tree takes upon itself more of its individual essence.

From a mature tree you can learn the resilience, flexibility, and acceptance that will strengthen your personal center. A mature tree can teach you how to call in the vision of what is unfolding so that you can maintain that personal center when there are unsettled conditions around you. In this way, you understand how to value self, and what you have to give the world through your being.

A very old tree undergoes another shift when its individual essence is completely merged with All That Is. An elder tree teaches you to be your Divine Self. You are without needing, without guilt or frustration because nothing matters except the Oneness of All Life. An elder tree can elevate you to the spiritual state where you have the capacity to look at all experiences in a very objective fashion, without any judgment. It is the space where you look at patterns of things, rather than at isolated experiences. From this vantage point you can observe the greater flow of what is taking place in life. You receive a greater knowledge of the sacredness of all life, and a deeper understanding that it is possible for all to live harmoniously, where nothing suffers at the expense of another.

Every Kingdom of Nature is in a cycle towards greater perfection of Self. As you perfect your Self, you can look to young trees for energy and emergence, mature trees for

stability, acceptance and patience, and elder trees for transcendence into Oneness. Honor your own spiritual nature,
and trust your guidance to lead you into Unity with All of
Life.

In our experience we have found no precise way to determine
the age of a tree. However, we have found that most trees you would
work with fall into the "mature" category. In a mature tree the individual species qualities are generally dominant. We have also found
that both the growth pattern of the species, as well as the geography
of the region affect the development of the tree's individuality. It
is possible to ask a tree Deva where the tree is in its life cycle. From
sensing the tree's connection to the divine, we can learn how Unconditional Love is expressed in our unique physical form. We can
also learn how it is refined and expanded throughout our spiritual
journey and finally, how it brings us into union with the Divine
Source.

FAMILY AND SPECIES PATTERNS

In this section we take a closer look at the spiritual qualities of
a tree species. These qualities are analogous to the qualities that
make us unique as an individual, such as one's outgoing nature, or
the ability to prioritize goals and carry them out.

One way that we have gained a broader understanding of family
and species qualities is through our work with flower essences.[1]
Flower essences are energized water made by placing flowers into
a container of purified water. When it is left in the sunlight, the life-
force energy of the flower activates the water. The essence is usually
preserved with alcohol and taken internally several drops at a time.

Our curiosity was stimulated by the fact that seventeen of the
thirty-eight Bach Flower Remedies are made from trees. We won-
dered whether taking Bach's Oak essence was the same as being near
the white oaks in Pennsylvania, where we were living at the time.
An intuitive comparison suggested that the energies were similar, but
not quite the same. We then compared the energy of the white oaks
to the energy of the red oaks which often grow together. Again, the
qualities were similar, but somewhat different. We perceived white
oak energy to be calm, steadfast, and enduring. Red oak, however,
seemed to introduce a more energizing resourcefulness. Both species were similar, however, in their quality of stable strength.

In our work with the trees we came to the conclusion that *a tree family will give an overall pattern of qualities. An individual species of that family will give a variation of the overall pattern.* In chapter seventeen we group the trees together by families, and summarize the overall family qualities, as well as the individual member qualities.

So what does this mean when you are in the woods and have decided that you wish to attune to the qualities of a tree? As we mentioned earlier, you must state your intent to work with the tree qualities. When you ask generally for balance, the tree will address that concern. If you wish to work with the tree species' qualities, you must ask a question that will yield those results. You can use the information in Part Two as a guide for asking questions.

The knowledge that an individual tree species can give a variation of an overall pattern of qualities can be very useful, especially to the neophytes of tree identification. For example, if you don't know what kind of oak or pine tree it is, you can attune to the overall qualities of the family. Secondly, when you are in a group of trees you can also consciously choose the one tree whose qualities you feel you most need. For instance when you are in the Sierra Nevada Mountains, you may need to choose from the Jeffrey, sugar, or ponderosa pine, as they frequently grow together.

The energy differences among the species can be quite subtle and difficult at first to perceive. It has taken Jonathan and me years to build our perception and sensitivities to tree energy. We have found that this journey has taken great patience and commitment, but yielded results far beyond our wildest dreams. Remember that trees as a part of creation want to be our friends and guides. They want to share their healing power and wisdom with us. They also want us to have full enjoyment of them in each season and in every stage of their lives.

8 | Developing Your Perceptions of Vibrational Frequencies

In THIS CHAPTER we explore three perspectives for discovering additional information on the spiritual qualities of trees: *sound, subtle body affinities* and the *four elements*. You can gain further insight into trees by sensing their energy fields from each of these perspectives. This is a process in which you focus upon what is happening to the energy in your body when you are in physical contact with the tree. Our beliefs influence the perceptions that we receive, and how we integrate our observations with other guidance from the trees.

SOUND

Everything in Nature, including trees and humans, has a dominant sound frequency that expresses spiritual qualities related to its highest purpose. This frequency is called its *soul tone*. *Toning* is the practice of making sounds with our voice for healing. The Douglas Fir Diva further describes the concept of the soul tone:

> A soul frequency is the purest essence of energy that is continually a part of the being, beyond its individuality. It does not change through incarnations but remains con-

stant. You might think of it as a band of frequencies that has the capacity to expand while at the same time maintaining its integrity. You of the human kingdom perceive this band of frequencies in a more limited way, as a single tone. Every lifestream has a soul tone that is the true identification of the being, an evolving blueprint that is independent of the individuality or personality that is being expressed during a given lifetime.

When you are seeking healing in the presence of a tree, you will receive an energy pattern that will bring the balance needed. This will not be the soul frequency, however. When you seek to understand in greater depth the spiritual nature of a particular tree, then you can ask to connect with its soul tone.

When you tone a tree with its soul tone, in that very instant you have entered that space of Total Knowing with that species. Your toning is received at the highest level of the tree's being, and it then communicates from that level with you.

Our experience with toning the soul frequency or soul tone, is that it works as a catalyst to elevate your Higher Conscious state so that you can perceive and understand from a broader perspective and with greater clarity. You can learn more about a tree's qualities by sounding its particular tone while in physical contact with it.

The effects of a tree's energy field on your own energy field are amplified by toning the soul frequency. When I find the right tone, I feel an "electric" charge energizing myself and the tree. It is as if the tree fully absorbs the soul tone, whereas a different frequency seems to "bounce off." It takes practice to become sensitive to sound within your body. However, it is a powerful tool for healing and is well worth the effort to cultivate.

You can use a pitch pipe or a musical instrument to label particular tones. A pitch pipe is the easiest instrument to use when you are in the woods. To loosen up your voice and get acquainted with making sounds and tones, try the following two exercises:

1. This first clearing exercise can be done anywhere and is good for the release of physical and emotional tension. Begin as low as you can go and make a sound like a siren, that moves up the scale as high as you can go, and back down again. Do this

several times and notice the reaction in your body. Do you feel a little lighter and more free?

2. Try making different tones and sounds and see which ones you like and which tones resonate or reverberate inside you. You might find yourself focusing on one tone, or making up a little tune. Notice whether your body feels more charged. You are making an intuitive connection with sound.

To find your particular soul tone, we have found it helpful to work in the range above high C. Look for a tone which creates a "current" connecting you to the Earth and to your Higher Self. It will resonate throughout your body and will feel both balancing and exhilarating.

To find the dominant frequency or soul tone for a tree, you can work in the normal range from middle C to high C and try the following four steps:

1. Become relaxed and clear your mind of preconceptions.
2. Become open and receptive, and attune yourself to the tree.
3. Make an initial tone using your pitch pipe, and be aware of how the tone resonates in your body and the tree.
4. How does it compare with your soul tone? Does it "harmonize" as though it were in the same pattern of frequency?

We give our perceptions of the soul tones in the discussions of the individual trees. I have noticed that a tree may resonate to more than one tone as it gives you the spiritual quality or frequency that you most need. These are like secondary tones that resonate to different aspects of the tree's qualities.

Trees and plants are known to respond on the physical level to certain sound frequencies. *The Secret Life of Plants* details a number of experiments where music as well as particular frequencies have increased plant growth. It is healing for the tree to hear its own soul tone. When you practice loving yourself and the tree through the use of sound, you may feel an uplifting energy charge through both yourself and the tree.

THE SUBTLE BODY AFFINITIES AND THE HUMAN ENERGY SYSTEM

We have stated earlier that everything in Nature, including humans, consists of life-force energy vibrating at different levels or frequencies, and is surrounded by an *energy field* or *aura*. The aura is a pattern or a template for the physical form.

Let us take a brief look at the part of your energy system that surrounds your body. The aura is composed of several layers or *subtle bodies* of increasingly finer frequencies. Our working system roughly defines three layers, which correspond to the physical, emotional-mental, and spiritual levels of development. We combine the emotional and mental levels together, as they both influence the creation of conscious beliefs. We have also grouped together several subtle bodies and referred to them as the "spiritual subtle body."

The physical layer is usually called the *etheric body* and extends out about one-quarter inch to two or three inches from the physical body. Being the densest layer, it is the easiest to perceive and is sometimes seen as a thin band of white or gray light. When you lean up against a tree, you are directly affecting the etheric body, which serves as a blueprint for the physical body.

Surrounding the etheric body are the *emotional and mental subtle bodies*. We sense these layers from three or four inches to about twelve inches above the body. These fields are often seen clairvoyantly as shimmering colors that indicate the emotional and mental state of a person's thoughts.

The *spiritual subtle body* extends from about twelve inches to about two or three feet from the physical body. This is the level in which you merge with your Higher Self and connect with the reality beyond your conscious, physical awareness.

Your subtle bodies are highly sensitive to thought forms. When a thought form enters one of your subtle bodies, the structure of that body changes to resonate with the thought. Depending on the nature of the thought, the subtle body either becomes more stable, structured, and filled with life-force energy, or more disorganized. This process happens very quickly and spontaneously with your passing thoughts. That is why clairvoyants often see many changing colors including predominant overtones. Your very being is structured by thoughts, therefore you can use positive thoughts to balance your sensitive energy fields.

In addition to serving as both a blueprint for the body and a record of your experience, the subtle bodies also serve as transducers of life-force energy. As you receive life-force energy from a variety of sources, including thought and tree energy, it is stepped down at each level and made into a grosser or denser form that your body can use.

If you wish to sense the energy field of a tree or trees without physical contact, try slowly walking in between two or more large trees, and see if you can sense when you walk into and out of the band of energy that connects the trees.

A small grouping of trees can be a powerful energy spot because of the geometric energy pattern that is set up with the particular placement of trees. You may notice this energy field if you are drawn intuitively to stand in a particular location. For this reason sacred groves of trees were used as places of worship in ancient times throughout the world.

In Part Two we have indicated which subtle bodies seem to be most activated by the tree. We did this by asking the Deva of the species for this information, and also by sensing the overall "density" of the energy. In general, we have a perception of "more density" when the emotional/mental level is energized. The energy of a tree that has an affinity with the spiritual subtle bodies seems to be more gentle and "ethereal." It also seems that the guidance from a tree that activates the spiritual subtle bodies is given from a broader perspective.

THE FOUR ELEMENTS

In order to better perceive the healing benefits of a tree, it can be helpful to observe its spiritual qualities from the perspective of the four Elements: Earth, Water, Fire and Air. How does the tree's energy *move* in your body? Is it fiery and activating (fire) or smooth and flowing (water)? Does it feel light and expanding (air) or centering and grounding (earth)?

In order to experience the qualities of the Four Elements in trees, we found it helpful to focus on the healing qualities of each element. The Elements heal on all levels because they are essential forms of life-force energy.

On the physical level you receive *Earth* energy from the foods you eat, helping to build your physical body. For this reason it is important to eat natural, unprocessed foods so that you receive the maximum amount of life-force energy.

Water is essential to maintain human life. In fact, your body is over 70% water. We can strengthen our etheric energy fields by taking water internally in the form of herbal teas. We also use water externally for cleansing.

Those who have practiced deep breathing as part of a transformational discipline know the revitalizing effects of the *air* we breathe. *Prana* is a Sanskrit term for breath and life-force energy. Pranayama, or regulated yogic breathing, is considered to be a gateway to expanded consciousness on all levels.

Sunlight is a source of vitamin D essential to human health, and certainly *fire* has played an essential role in cooking our food and keeping warm.

The Elements can teach you about your spiritual purpose in life. By attuning with each Element, you can affirm being in harmony with Nature. By determining which Element seems most meaningful to you, and connecting with a tree with that particular attunement, you can receive guidance about the direction to take in your growth.

From the Earth Element you can learn to accept the sacred responsibility that you have as a steward for your own body, as well as for our precious earth. You learn how to properly and continuously align your energies with the Earth so that you can maintain a centeredness and balance as you follow your own path. As with all of the Elements, you come to appreciate the beauty and perfection of the smallest forms of life you see on Earth. If you feel that your energies are scattered in too many directions, connecting with a tree with Earth attunement can help you give more attention to your present space. *Earth qualities are deepening, centering, focusing, and stabilizing.*

By attuning with the Water Element you can perceive ways to integrate your level of sensitivity through the use of the emotional body. It can help you let go of conditional responses to life experiences, and move towards Unconditional Love and greater acceptance of self and others. It also allows you to understand the aspect of feeling which exists beyond the physical level and to greatly expand your senses. When you are either overstimulated by your feelings or cut off from your feelings, connecting with a tree with a water attunement will help you cleanse your emotional body. *Water qualities are flowing, surrendering, harmonizing and accepting.*

By attuning with Air you learn how to be spiritually mindful and to utilize the energies of the mind for the highest good of all concerned. You move from a space of "me-ness" to one of Universality. A tree with an air attunement can assist you in clearing mental or spiritual confusion. Air energies are *detaching, clarifying and uplifting.*

By aligning with Fire you learn a purposeful focus of the life-force energy, referred to as power. You learn how to take a concept and give it greater clarity through proper use of your mind and will. A tree with a fire attunement can act as a catalyst, assisting you in burning your reluctance to take the necessary steps in your growth. *Fire qualites are purifying, stimulating, expansive and action-oriented.*

The Elements of Earth, Water, Air and Fire (sun) are necessary for both your physical and spiritual life.

We have looked at sound, the subtle bodies, and the Four Elements as ways of deepening our understanding about the spiritual qualities of trees (and other forms of Nature). In Part Two you will find our perceptions of the soul tone, the subtle body affinities, and resonating elements for each tree, in the section entitled "Spiritual Aspects."

PART TWO

Descriptions of the Individual Trees

The first stop on our cross-country tree visiting was a state park in Nebraska. We chased after the park ranger more than once with a handful of fallen leaves, in order to ask for his help in identification.

Finally the seventy-year-old ranger remarked, "You know, some people might think you folks are a bit weird being tree nuts and all. But one thing I've learned in all my years, and that is, you can't get closer to God than nature. Now me, I like to fish myself. I just love to . . ." and he chattered on about his love for fishing.

You can't get closer to God than Nature. I knew that his simple statement was a sign of confirmation that the Devas were with us at the start of our personal adventure.

In Part Two the trees are grouped in chapters according to the area in which we observed them, or where they grow most prolifically or to their largest size. For example, although you can find ponderosa pine west of the Rockies and all the way to the Cascades and the Sierras, it is a dominant feature of the Rocky Mountain forest and is therefore given in that chapter.

This book is not intended to be a definite identification guidebook, because we are not naturalists or botanists. Therefore we strongly encourage you to utilize guidebooks and other resources in making tree identifications. If identifying trees seems like a difficult task, you are in good company:

> An important fact to appreciate is that precise identification is not always possible and sometimes is a matter of opinion based on weighing the relative importance of conflicting facts. For example, a Red Oak can be described as having ten or more specific features which, together, identify a tree as a Red Oak. However, in practice, one seldom finds an Oak that has all these features. It is more likely that a particular tree will have only some of them, while other details will be those characteristic of another Oak. It is thus apparent that only by deciding which features seem most important can the tree be placed in a somewhat dubious category. This responsibility rests with the botanist, and there are often honest differences of opinion on these matters.

> This curious situation should not deter the amateur—on the contrary, it simplifies his problem. Precise identification is not only debatable but totally unnecessary for a full enjoyment of trees . . .[1]

We also apologize to those of you who find that your favorite trees are not given in this book. We hope that our work will encourage you to find out more about their qualities for yourself. Also, you can work with qualities of a related species, as we discussed in chapter seven.

We first give the most common name of the tree, followed by local name variations. Latin names serve the purpose of providing an identification system that is uniform worldwide. The name of a genus or family such as *Quercus* (Oak) is listed first, followed by the species name *alba* (white). So *Quercus alba* is understood as White Oak. A key word or phrase is a guide to our perceptions of the nature of its qualities.

The section on *Physical Aspects* and the illustration will give you further clues on identifying the tree. The *Species Deva* then communicates about the spiritual qualities of the tree, and additional perspectives are given in the *Spiritual Aspects* section.

In *Co-creating* we relate other insights we have discovered or highlight qualities that have been most meaningful for us in our everyday lives. Our communication with the tree ends with an affirmation which you can use as part of your process of opening to the tree, as well as afterwards to help you maintain your new state of balance. Take time to read from areas of the country other than your own, as the Devas offer much wisdom. And who knows what trees might inspire you to visit them in person! We hope you enjoy your armchair journey as you read, as well as your own forest experiences.

9 | Trees of the Pacific Northwest

ON OUR FIRST trip to the Northwest to find an apartment, we searched for the nearest state park in order to be with the trees. As we climbed the path up a short ridge, the first thing we noticed was the unusual fragrance—a lush smell of dampness and decay that seemed to speak of rain, mosses, ferns and great fertility.

These ancient forests extended along the Pacific coast from southern Alaska to central California. In Washington and Oregon they are bounded by the western slopes of the Cascades. This region is characterized by moderate temperatures and wet winters, which are ideal conditions for the growth of very large trees. Many of these trees easily reach seventy-five to one-hundred feet and are from one to three feet or more in diameter.

These woods are like a natural cathedral, cool and peaceful. The eye is carried upward along the giant trunks to the protective cover of the branches above. Because we live here now, these are the trees that nurture us on a daily basis, so we have a special love for them. You will find most of the trees in this chapter in the lowlands of western Washington and Oregon, and the lower elevations of Olympic, Rainier, and Cascades National Parks. Pacific silver fir is a tree of the western mountain slopes from two thousand to five thousand feet and is quite common in the national parks.

WESTERN RED CEDAR

Giant Arborvitae, Canoe Cedar
Thuja plicata

Quality: Self-Determination

Physical Aspects

America does not have a true native cedar, and the term "cedar" actually covers members of the juniper, arborvitae, and cypress families. Western red cedar is one of the giants of the Pacific coast lowland forests, and is found from southeast Alaska to northwestern California. Western red cedar also grows in the northern Rockies in Idaho and Montana.

Like the arborvitae shrub, Western red cedar's shiny, green scale-like leaves look as though they have been ironed flat. The cinnamon red-brown bark is tough and stringy, and both the leaves and the wood are quite fragrant. Tiny, brown elliptical cones about one-half-inch long grow in clusters, upright from a small stock.

The Western Red Cedar Deva:

The *will* synthesizes your spiritual awareness, your thoughts and your emotions, and the physical vehicle is activated to manifest this synthesis. Your will then becomes an expression of your being at a given time. Sometimes you may have felt that your life is being controlled by the actions of others, or you may have been told that you do not have the ability to do what you wish to do in your life. When your own personal thoughts and feelings become clouded with imbalanced thought patterns from other beings, there can be confusion, frustration, and pain in your life. So rather than moving forward on your path, you may feel reluctance or dread about taking a particular action.

My purpose is to help you find clarity from within self, rather than from others. I teach you to know your own inner strength and your own inner boundaries. I help you to recognize the power that you have to make the necessary changes of the moment. Then you can go forth without hesitation or a sense of restriction, and do what you need to do.

Spiritual Aspects

Soul Tone: C#
Subtle Body Affinities: Emotional/Mental
Element: Fire

Co-creating with Western Red Cedar

Cedar energy can help strengthen and purify your will. One of the reasons that cedar smoke may have been used for purification by Native Americans is because it can help you release anger, frustration or reluctance related to excessive influence from others. It also strengthens your courage and determination to pursue your tasks. If you have difficulty motivating yourself to carry out a direction in your personal growth, Western red cedar activates your determination to move beyond self-doubts. It is therefore a confidence-builder, encouraging you to look to your own inner resources for personal power.

Affirmation

"My own inner strength guides me, and my next step becomes clear, as I release the influence of others in determining my actions."

DOUGLAS FIR

Oregon Pine, Douglas Spruce, Douglas Yew
Pseudotsuga menziesii

Quality: Honoring Your Gifts

Physical Aspects

Douglas fir is truly a magnificent tree with a majestic stature and graceful boughs. It is not a true fir because its cones hang down from the branches rather than remaining upright as they do on true firs. The Douglas fir cone is easily identifiable because it has three-pronged tongues sticking out between the scales. Its bark is also very distinctive with its heavy vertical ridges and thick gray plates. Douglas fir needles are gray-green, flattened, and blunt, like hemlock needles. However, these needles are longer, ranging from one-half to one-and-one-half inches long, and they grow all around the twig, giving the tree a bushy, lush appearance.

There are two geographical varieties of Douglas fir. The tall, Pacific coast variety lives on moist, well-drained soil in the lowland forests from central British Columbia to central California. The Rocky Mountain variety (*Pseudotsuga menziesii var. glauca*) likes drier rocky soils and ranges all through the Rocky Mountains to about two thousand feet in elevation in the north to ninety-five hundred feet in the south.

The Douglas Fir Deva

My message to the Human Kingdom continues to be to believe in yourself. You are a unique creation of Spiritual Divinity, with infinite creative possibilities. I encourage you to take stock of your personal resources, and honor your gifts and those qualities that are unique to yourself. In this way you align yourself with your flow and purpose in life and affirm yourself not only in terms of the outer world but in terms of the growth taking place inside you.

I wish to speak to you about pride. Pride does not say, ''I am better than you,'' or ''The ways I have of working in the world are more significant than yours.'' Pride is not jealous of the accomplishments of others. Rather, pride blesses others in whatever they are doing as well as what the self has accomplished. Pride does not say, ''Oh, I never had to work through that,'' or ''I'm beyond that,'' to another who is undergoing difficulties. Pride has compassion for the struggles of others. Pride honors the space of all forms of life. To feel more at peace, you can release the excessive demands of pride. In that way you will feel more at home with your growth. Work with the power of positive expectations by including the words, ''for my Highest Good.'' Then striving for achievement becomes working towards fulfillment.

Spiritual Aspects

Soul Tone: E
Subtle Body Affinities: Emotional/Mental
Element: Air/Earth

Co-creating with Douglas Fir

Douglas fir's special teaching is how to enjoy your uniqueness and build your self-confidence, without being stuck in the trap of excessive ego, or pride. When you belittle yourself, doubt your abilities, or feel insignificant, Douglas fir helps you stand tall and affirm your attributes or talents. On the other hand, if your ego gets out of hand, Douglas fir teaches you about humility. It activates a quality of self-reliance and a quiet pride that looks inside for self-definition rather than to others, so that you go about your business with poise and self-esteem.

The energy of Douglas fir seems to realign the back in such a manner that you feel as though you are indeed standing taller.

Affirmation

"I stand tall and honor my gifts with a spiritual sense of self."

GRAND FIR

Lowland White Fir, Yellow Fir
Abies grandis

Quality: Becoming Aware of Subconscious Emotional Wounds

Physical Aspects

The fir family is widely distributed in North America and can be identified in three ways. First, the cones stand straight up on the branches rather than hanging down, as is the case with Douglas fir. Secondly, when you twist a needle off the twig, it leaves a round scar flat on the twig. Finally, fir bark is often covered with blisters of fragrant resin.

The tallest fir is the grand fir, found in the lowland forests from British Columbia to California and in the Rockies to central Idaho. It is perhaps most plentiful in Oregon. It can be difficult to distinguish grand fir from Douglas fir, particularly because grand fir is not as common. Grand fir bark is gray or brown, with shallower ridges and smaller plates than Douglas fir. You may also find more resin blisters on the bark.

The shiny green needles are one-and-one-quarter to two inches long, and grow in two flat rows on either side of the twig, like hemlock needles. Douglas fir needles are shorter, more slender, and they grow all around the twig. The grand fir needles are whitish below, and have a "grapefruity" fragrance.

The ground around a Douglas fir will usually be littered with cones, but you will find few if any cones under a grand fir. The scales fall off the yellow-green cones on a grand fir when the seeds are ripe, and the cones then disintegrate on the tree.

Grand Fir Deva

From the time you were very young, you have been taught that it is wrong for you to express what you are feeling inside. When you do not acknowledge or express painful feelings when they occur, the energy of those feelings remains stored in your subconscious memory, and in the very cells of your body. A current experience can trigger the energy of stored emotions so that you may not understand why an emotion is present.

My energies can help you go back in time to the moment when the original experience occurred, so that you can better understand the feelings that were attached to it. I share with you what needs to be healed inside, so that you can then disconnect from the past experience.

Once you better understand the hidden facets of an issue, my energies can aid you in seeing where change can be instigated. Instead of saying, ''I should have known better or I wouldn't be in this particular state,'' you learn through me not to judge, but rather to accept what is revealed to you so that you can heal.

Throughout this process, trust that what you are feeling in any given moment is real to you, and not a product of your imagination. Your emotional body, when you listen to it, gives you the gift of honesty.

My energies can teach you to value your emotional nature as a way of understanding your spirituality. When you move from the space of fear to one of Unconditional Love through the unfoldment of your emotional being, then you become more receptive to the energies of your spiritual body. Your emotional sensitivity becomes a springboard for your spiritual evolution.

Spiritual Aspects

Soul Tone: A
Subtle Body Affinities: Emotional/Mental
Element: Water/Fire

Co-creating with Grand Fir

Grand Fir energy goes deep, bringing to your awareness emotions and beliefs that you have hidden from conscious awareness because they are painful. This energy is particularly useful for understanding how early childhood traumas and limiting beliefs are affecting you now. When working with grand fir, you can ask the following questions:

1.   What is causing me to feel the pain that I am feeling now? The energy may feel a little unpleasant, depending on the intensity of your feelings.
2.   What do I need to affirm that helps me accept your Unconditional Love? Allow the awareness of your feelings to remain present, and gift yourself with acceptance and compassion.

For example, I sought out grand fir to help me understand why I felt sad about a particular incident. The sense I got was one of self-dislike, which at first surprised me because I thought that I had worked through the worst of those feelings. I then asked, "How old am I?" and got an image of a little girl, age seven or eight, who felt very insecure and alone. I affirmed to my little girl that she was indeed good enough and that I loved, accepted and admired her. As I worked with the affirmation/image, I noticed a gradual releasing of a burden. I thanked the grand fir and continued on my walk with a sense of lightness and freedom that seems to be a special gift of the fir family.

Affirmation
"I choose now to become aware of and to release old burdens."

PACIFIC SILVER FIR

Lovely Fir
Abies Amabilis

Quality: Releasing Current Emotional Upsets

Physical Aspects

The Latin "amabilis" means "lovely fir" and Pacific silver fir is indeed a beautiful tree. It is a tree of the North, where it grows in Alaska and all through the Cascades of Washington and Oregon. It is the most common fir in the Olympic and Mt. Rainier National Parks.

Pacific silver fir has light gray bark with white patches, like the bark of red alder. The needles point upward toward the end of the twig and the green topside of the needle contrasts with the white underside. Pacific silver fir has upright purplish-brown cones and the resinous blisters that are typical of the fir family.

The Pacific Silver Fir Deva

I help you understand and release emotions of the immediate moment, relating to your daily activities. When you are reluctant to look at a particular experience that has emotionally upset you, you are giving power to a painful feeling. Its very strength will ultimately deplete your life-force energies. A feeling can be seen as an energy with no attachments to it. When you let go of judging yourself for feeling a certain way, the energy shifts and the intensity diffuses so that you can work with the feeling in a positive manner. A painful feeling is a plea for your attention.

Sometimes what is needed is time so that you can assimilate the wisdom from an experience. I teach you patience and acceptance to allow what you can do in the moment, to be. Sometimes waiting is as much an important part of the solution as any action that you may take.

I can also help you step back from an experience in order to become the observer. From a more detached vantage point you can then clarify whether the painful emotion signals a deeper conflict within you, or whether some conflict within the other person is triggering a response in you.

I teach you to move into a space of clarity in your emotions so that all levels of your being remain centered. A wonderful gift that you give through your presence is emotional sensitivity and balance. A gift you can give to yourself is a natural flow of peace.

Spiritual Aspects

Soul Tone: A
Subtle Body Affinities: Emotional/Mental
Element: Water/Fire

Co-creating with Pacific Silver Fir

Pacific silver fir aids you in releasing daily upsets, such as having a flat tire, that may relate to deeper issues. Pacific silver fir helps to focus your attention on feelings and beliefs which need to be recognized rather than rationalized or ignored. While grand fir can help you understand what the core issues are, Pacific silver fir helps you with the release of the accompanying emotional pain. It teaches you to release blame and judgment so that you can feel cleansed, pure and free like the mountain air where Pacific silver fir grows.

Affirmation

"I release the events of my day and surround myself and others with purification and love."

WESTERN HEMLOCK

Tsuga heterophylla

Quality: Faith

Physical Aspects

Western hemlock is one of the towering giants of the Pacific coast forest along with Douglas fir and Western red cedar. It ranges from southern Alaska to northwestern California and is also found in the northern Rockies of Idaho and Montana. Western hemlock is a companion to the sitka spruce, the dominant tree of the temperate rain forest on the Olympic peninsula.

Western hemlock needles are blunt, flat, and dark green above, with two whitish bands below. At one-half-inch long, they are shorter than either Douglas fir or grand fir needles and they grow in two rows along the twig. The elliptical, brown cones are also about one-half-inch long and they dangle from the tips of the twigs. These cones are more pointed than those of the Eastern hemlock. If you ever get to see the top of the tree, you will notice that the top twelve inches or so flop over.

Western Hemlock Deva

I wish to speak to you about change and the flow of events in your life. It is easy for you to desire that events take place exactly when you want them; however, this is seeing life from the point of reference of a fixed reality. When an unexpected or difficult experience occurs, I help you to move beyond either avoiding or attacking the experience out of frustration. Balance comes from staying in the moment with an experience and working creatively through it. I ask you to accept changing circumstances and be open to how you can benefit from a challenging experience. *Faith* becomes knowing that the way to master a difficult circumstance is to look for all the learning possibilities that an experience holds.

If, however, you appear to be on a plateau, and life seems boring and monotonous, it is an indication that you have not examined all the major facets of an experience. My energies help you to lift boredom, so that you can find more aspects of an experience from which to grow.

It is true that changes have intensified in your present space and time. It is not so much a matter of how fast experiences flow into and through your life; rather it is how creatively you assimilate your experiences.

Whatever the flow of events in your life, I can reassure you that the present space is transitory. When you acknowledge that growth is occurring through the change process, you will find balance within, and you will be richer than you could have imagined.

Spiritual Aspects

Soul Tone: F
Subtle Body Affinities: Emotional/Mental
Element: Water

Co-creating with Western Hemlock

Both Western and Eastern hemlock develop your understanding of faith as you confront the process of change. Faith is related to trusting that you can learn something valuable from every experience, even the difficult ones. Western hemlock is particularly helpful in reducing the shock or immobility that may accompany traumatic circumstances. When you ask the question, "Why is this happening to me?" Western hemlock says, "Trust and be as open as you can to the experience even though you don't see the whole picture." If you deny that you have the capacity to work with an experience, Western hemlock reassures you that you indeed have the tools to deal with it.

Western hemlock energy is like a flowing stream that says that everything changes. Therefore it aids you in letting go of the desire that things be like they were in the past. When you are feeling the pain of separation from others, hemlock returns your focus to the present moment, making it easier to let go of the experience with more equanimity and balance.

Affirmation

"My faith increases as I trust the Light."

SITKA SPRUCE

Picea sitchensis

Quality: Understanding Your Spiritual Purpose

Physical Aspects

Sitka spruce grows from Alaska to the redwoods of California, along the mild, foggy areas of the Pacific coast. It is the tree most associated with the temperate rain forest on the western side of the Olympics in Washington.

Sitka spruce needles are dark green and flat, unlike other needles of the spruce family, and they grow all around the twig. However, they are quite pointed, which distinguishes them from the blunt fir needles. The bark of the spruce family is distinctive, with dark brown scales rather than the vertical furrows of Western hemlock or Douglas fir. The cones are light brown, cylindrical and two- to three-and-one-half inches long, and they hang at the end of the twig. Sitka spruce often grows from a broad base and the roots may protrude, which distinguishes it from other cedars and firs.

Sitka Spruce Deva

So often I've heard humans say, ''I do not know what my spiritual purpose is,'' or ''I really don't think that I am accomplishing my spiritual purpose in life.'' How do you know if you are accomplishing your spiritual purpose? When you experience a sense of peace inside, and a feeling of inner connection with what you are doing, then you know that you are on your path. Finding a deeper meaning in your activities beyond a surface enjoyment, is what connects you with your spiritual purpose.

Sometimes you may become discouraged, as a result of seeing your spiritual purpose from too narrow a perspective. For example, let's say that your spiritual service has to do with working in a healing capacity for other beings. In order to effectively work with others, you must work on yourself, so that you can be a more powerful channel. You must learn patience, and compassion for your fellow humans, and for other life forms as well. So when you feel that you are drifting from your spiritual purpose, my energies can help you to understand the connection between your experiences and your spiritual path.

I encourage steadfastness when you are in a period of uncertainty, because my energies affirm that you are on your path whether or not you receive recognition along this path. When your connection to your spirituality is strengthened, the affairs of the material world are not so confusing.

I can also help you clarify and refine your spiritual purpose. If, for example, you know that you are to do healing work, I can help you clarify what type of healing work is appropriate.

When you need to know whether or not you have made a major shift from your spiritual course, I deepen your recommitment to your particular service. When your mental body is aligned with your service, then your Higher Consciousness can infuse you with life-force energy, so that balance is restored and the expression of your service can continue in its natural pattern.

Spiritual Aspects

Soul Tone: C
Subtle Body Affinities: Mental, Spiritual
Element: Fire/Earth

Co-creating with Sitka Spruce

When you feel discouraged or disillusioned about whether or not you are fulfilling your spiritual purpose, Sitka spruce offers a very affirmative recommitment to your process. For example, you might have a part- or full-time job to support you while you do your personal healing work. You wonder if this is really what you need to be doing. Sitka spruce helps you to feel more at peace, as you become aware of the broader, affirmative picture. If you are unclear or uncertain, Sitka spruce can help you clarify your spiritual goals and prioritize the steps that you need to take along your path. Sitka spruce energy strengthens your dedication, tenacity, and patience, encouraging you to be a lighthouse in your world.

Affirmation

"My inner insight reassures me that I am living my spiritual purpose."

PACIFIC MADRONE

Arbutus menzieii

Quality: Stewardship

Physical Aspects

Pacific madrone is the tallest American member of the evergreen, heath family which includes rhododendrons, azaleas and blueberries. Its thick, glossy leaves grow two- to four-and-one-half inches long and look like rhododendron leaves. Perhaps madrone's most outstanding feature is its bark, which is red with green, yellow or brown patches. Pacific madrone has sap chemicals which permeate the bark layers so that each layer takes on a different color. The bark peels in patches, revealing the different colors. Pacific madrone bears white, urn-shaped flowers in clusters, which appear on the ends of twigs in the spring. In the fall they are transformed into showy, orange-red berries, reminiscent of mountain ash berries. Pacific madrone stands out in any season of the year.

Look for Pacific madrone from British Columbia to central California. You will also find it in the Sierra Nevada mountains.

Pacific Madrone Deva

I teach you about the wise use of resources. The material forms around you are a part of your resources. How do you decide how much money to have and what to buy? For example, do you choose to purchase an additional automobile to raise your self-esteem in the eyes of others? Do you worry about material lack in your life? Do you feel that the "right possession" will make you happy? This is the "just one more" pattern.

When you have more possessions around you than you need, they become a burden. More and more of your life-force energy must be directed toward the maintenance of your possessions, and you become focused on paths that are not truly enhancing your growth and spiritual service.

One way of evaluating your possessions is to ask whether a possession fills your space with Light, in some way. If so, then it is fulfilling its purpose in being with you. Sometimes it happens that a possession brings Light for a period of time, and in so doing, fulfills its purpose. Then it is time to let it go.

Another question you can ask yourself in evaluating your wise use of possessions is, "How much time do I devote to my spirituality?" If your answer is, "I really don't have time for it," then you can take that as an indication that you need to reassess the excess burdens that you are carrying.

Your own life-force energy is another valuable resource. When you live the quality of practicality, you are
continually asking yourself, "What are my priorities and
how much energy do I need to spend on each step?"
"How can I best utilize the energy resources at hand to
complete a particular process in which I am involved?"

Pain occurs when you judge your present space or
your rate of progress toward particular goals. I help you to
find meaning and worth in what you are doing so that you
learn how to pace yourself more effortlessly, and how to
better appreciate what you accomplish along your path.

Wise use of resources is the basis for balance on the
Earth Plane. Wastefulness and overextension of life-force
energies weigh you down. When you utilize only the energy
needed you create more balance within Self and also within
the Kingdoms of Nature.

Spiritual Aspects

Soul Tone: C#
Subtle Body Affinities: Emotional/Mental
Element: Earth

Co-creating with Pacific Madrone

Pacific madrone can bring a sense of comfort and acceptance,
when the fulfillment of a goal seems to be taking a long time. If your
tendency is to run rampant and scatter your energies, Pacific
madrone encourages you to slow down and work in a practical, focused, organized fashion. With Pacific madrone you can better understand how to move from extravagance to moderation in your use
of your outer resources as well as your time.

Affirmation

"I release any imbalance that clutters my knowing of what I truly
need present in my physical and mental space."

RED ALDER

Western Alder
Alnus rubra

Quality: Joy

Physical Aspects

Red alder is a pioneer on ground that has been burned or logged. It also likes the damp lowlands and streambanks of the coastal region from southeastern Alaska to central California. Alder is a medium-sized tree of fifty to one hundred feet.

Its bark is a distinctive smooth gray, with patches of white, giving it a mottled appearance. Look for dark green leaves with wavy margins and double sawteeth. Leaves are gray-green underneath with reddish rusty hairs, and the edges often curl under. Spring brings yellowish catkins that are four to six inches long. In late summer you will begin to find the small, dark cones, about three-quarters of an inch long, that usually remain attached to the tree.

Red Alder Deva

Your world has taught you to be reserved in what you feel and think. My energies encourage your outward expression of exuberance. Allow your enthusiasm and spontaneity to flow unimpeded from one moment to the next. In this way you create pure joy, and freedom to express yourself through your creative energies.

The power in being lies in seeking the newness of each moment. If you feel that you have exhausted all the possible ways that you can work with a situation, I bring you a fresh perspective that broadens your viewpoint. As you expand your horizons to find creative solutions, you will have a better sense of timing for any changes that need to be made.

I teach you how to find joy and to Be JOY. Joy and spontaneity go hand in hand. When you act spontaneously you can find something good in the present moment which can restore faith in yourself and a sense of meaning in your life. You will find that you are more resilient than you ever thought you could be.

Look for the ''happy center'' in each moment and the humor in your circumstances. Don't wait until the weekend to feel good. There is no pain in the immediate moment because every moment is a new beginning for laughter, joy and Light.

Spiritual Aspects

Soul Tone: E
Subtle Body Affinities: Emotional/Mental
Element: Fire

Co-creating with Red Alder

Red alder energy has a quality of innocent, child-like enthusiasm that is both stimulating and cheerful. It offers an outpouring of energy that insists that you get on with life and open your eyes to the beauty around you. Seek out red alder when you feel depressed, overly serious, or find yourself dwelling on the past. Red alder turns up the music, sets your toes to tapping, and before you know it, you are dancing into the future.

Affirmation

"The power in being lies in seeking the newness of each moment."

BLACK COTTONWOOD

Western Balsam Poplar
Populus trichocarpa

Quality: Bringing Spirit Into Body

Physical Aspects

Black cottonwood is the tallest broadleaf tree in the Pacific Northwest, as well as the largest member of the American poplar family. With a height of sixty to one hundred twenty feet and a diameter of one to three feet, it continues its pioneer reputation as a sentinel of the West. Although black cottonwood is found in the moist lowlands from Alaska to Oregon, it also extends into the drier areas of southern California, the Sierra Nevadas, and the Rockies of Idaho and Montana. In these drier areas, it grows where its roots can capture moisture from streams or marshes.

Black cottonwood's leaves are a leathery, shiny green, with fine, wavy teeth. They are easily distinguishable from the leaves of its most frequent companions, bigleaf maple and red alder. Black cottonwood is a prolific spreader whose stumps sprout readily. Like willow, cottonwood twigs that are planted in wet ground will grow into new trees.

Black cottonwoods bear male and female flowers on separate trees. The female flowers mature into clusters of fruit. When the fruiting capsules split open in the summer, the seeds become airborne amid a cottony fluff, which gives the tree its name.

Black Cottonwood Deva

I help you to see that your physical vehicle is a mirror reflection of the perfection of your divine essence. When you know this to be true, there is less need for judging how your physical vehicle is responding to your needs in the present moment. You can then affirm the rightness of your physical vehicle for your work in this life. There are many of you who have had a reluctance to remain fully connected to your physical vehicle while on the Earth Plane. Your memory of being in the spirit body, with its purity and lightness, reinforces a stronger attachment or desire to be back in that space. My energies help you to see how your physical vehicle supports your spiritual growth so that you can continue your commitment to learn what you came onto the Earth Plane to learn.

As you observe the perfect evolution of physical form and spirit that unfolds in Nature, so this evolution unfolds in the Human Kingdom as well. The more that you open to this process within your own being, the more the Divine flow will manifest through you.

Spiritual Aspects

Soul Tone: C
Subtle Body Affinities: Spiritual
Element: Water/Earth

Co-creating with Black Cottonwood

The cottonwood family teaches you about the sacredness of your physical body. When you have been wishing that you had someone else's physical characteristics, black cottonwood reminds you of the joy and beauty of the physical forms on this planet, especially your own. If you are experiencing any kind of physical limitation or imbalance, black cottonwood affirms your opportunity to learn about Unconditional Love, and reassures you about your journey. If you have ever wished that you weren't even in a physical body, the grounded safety and comfort of black cottonwood can help focus your attention on the present moment, and the goodness of being alive.

Affirmation

"My physical body is a mirror of my Divine Essence."

BIGLEAF MAPLE

Acer macrophyllum

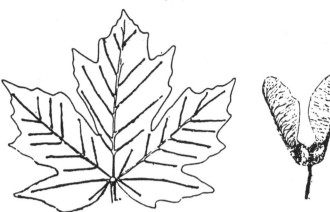

Quality: Interconnectedness with All of Life

Physical Aspects

Bigleaf maple is accurately named, with leaves often as large as dinner plates. The leaves have five lobes, with deep indentations between each lobe, and the distinctive maple shape. You will find bigleaf maple shading the moist soils of the Pacific coast from Alaska to southern California, and they are especially lovely in the Puget Sound region of Washington.

The thinly furrowed, gray to reddish brown bark is often covered with moss and ferns. Small, yellow, fragrant flowers appear with the leaves in the spring. The winged seeds characteristic of maple hang in furry yellow clusters all summer long, and they mature in the fall.

Bigleaf Maple Deva

Before you came onto the Earth Plane, you knew your Unity and Oneness with All of Life. When you came onto the Earth Plane, you were exposed to programs that spoke of separateness from others, and now you sometimes forget your own Unity with Unconditional Love. When you allow other lifestreams to become true mirror reflections of your own Spiritual Divinity, then you reawaken your awareness of your own Inner Essence. Your goal is to enter into your relationships with a pure heart, seeking to expand your understanding and truth. Look in terms of what is working well in another's process and integrate that understanding into your life. You heal and are healed as you extend the purity of your Unconditional Love to others.

When you feel disappointed or discouraged, my energies affirm to you that Nature truly listens to your call for comfort and your need for understanding. Through me you can learn how to give and receive from others. You build upon your truth from understanding your relationships with all of life.

Spiritual Aspects

Soul Tone: D
Subtle Body Affinities: Spiritual
Element: Air

Co-creating with Bigleaf Maple

Like other trees of the maple family, bigleaf maple supports you in learning to give and receive love from others. It is easier to let go of loneliness or feelings of abandonment or disappointment when you are able to connect with the Unconditional Love in Nature and the Divinity in your human friends. Bigleaf maple teaches you about the interconnectedness of all life, and helps you to enjoy the pleasures of your environment. You are always welcomed home next to her gnarled, mossy trunk, and comforted under her friendly shade. Her bigness lifts you above feeling separate and into the space where Unconditional Love flows into your heart and spirit again.

Affirmation

"I learn to give and receive Unconditional Love so that others know the presence of that Divine Love within themselves."

10 | Trees of California

CALIFORNIA IS NOTED for its diversity of trees, partly because of the variety of terrain. Two mountain ranges extend the length of the state; the Pacific coastal range on the west, and the Sierra Nevada mountains, which are an extension of the Cascade range, on the east. In between the two mountain chains are the plains and valleys which have their own unique trees, as well as numerous plantings.

The Sierra Nevada range is a meeting ground of diverse climates and includes trees from the Pacific coast such as Douglas fir, and bigleaf maple. You will also find ponderosa pine, lodgepole pine, and quaking aspen from the Rockies, which we will describe later.

When we drove through California for the fist time, we were delighted with the numerous ornamental trees. However, our guidance was that we were to encourage people to discover the native forests, so we have included only a few cultivated trees in a later chapter. An entire book could be written about California trees alone, and we hope that California natives will be inspired to attune with many more of the California trees.

In this chapter we will first describe two coastal trees, the Redwood and coast live oak. Then we will travel inland with valley oak and the eucalyptus. We end our California survey in the Sierra Nevada mountains where you will meet the dominant trees that we saw when visiting the Lake Tahoe region and Sequoia National Park.

COASTAL REDWOOD

California Redwood, Sequoia
Sequoia sempervirens

Quality: The Inspiration of Transcendence

Physical Aspects

There are two kinds of sequoias in this country, the coastal redwood, and the giant sequoia. Redwoods are the tallest trees in the world, averaging two hundred to three hundred twenty-five feet in height, and ten to sixteen feet in diameter. The oldest known redwood is over two thousand years old. The name "redwood" probably comes from the fact that the wood is a pinky-red when it is first exposed to air, before it turns a reddish-brown.

Redwoods grow in the fog belt along the Pacific coast from southwestern Oregon to Monterey, California, where they receive fifty to sixty inches of annual rainfall.

The needles somewhat resemble fir or hemlock needles and are of two kinds. The ones along the branches are in two rows and are about an inch long. The needles on the growth tips are much smaller, at one-fourth inch long, and they spread around the twig.

Redwood cones are tiny in comparison to the tree. They are about one inch long with reddish-brown furrows. Unlike other conifers, sprouts can grow from the stumps of the redwood tree, and they reach tree size after a few years.

When you are in a redwood grove, you can lose all sense of sound, space and time, and it is like being in the presence of infinity.

Coastal Redwood Deva

When you face adversity, you have a choice as to what effect that condition has upon your present space. I tell you that you have a tremendous capacity for the renewal of your will to live and be, no matter what the condition. I help you to move beyond your emotional and mental awareness, to understanding your experience from a spiritual perspective. When you elevate your consciousness into the spiritual dimension, you have the ability to see that experience as finite, in an infinite field of opportunities.

Growth is a time-consuming process. It is gradual and steady, and occurs as more and more of the elements appear to facilitate that growth. Your experiences in life are similar to the elements that I require for my growth. They are the necessary fuel that you need in order to take your next step. Aspiration is moving through your life toward something greater than yourself, always living to the fullest that you know.

As you evolve on your spiritual path, you seek greater understanding of Unconditional Love. Learn to share the common resource of this life-force energy that exists all around you, for when you do, all life benefits. Everything that exists has its unique purpose in being and when this pupose is allowed to express itself completely, a Higher Purpose is fulfilled. The fulfillment of your being interweaves with the particular growth pattern for Planet Earth. Your presence is blessed in this space, because LOVE IS AND ALWAYS WILL BE.

Spiritual Aspects

Soul Tone: High C
Subtle Body Affinities: Spiritual, Emotional/Mental
Element: Fire

Co-creating with Coastal Redwood

If you feel insignificant or defeated, coastal redwood inspires you to believe in a Plan greater than yourself. You can also renew your sense of faith in the power of Unconditional Love. Redwood aids you in dissolving fears about death or tragedy, supporting your transcendence of finite experiences. With coastal redwood, you are carried up high, to merge with the stars.

Affirmation

"I merge with Unconditional Love, to become Greater than myself."

COAST LIVE OAK

California Live Oak, Encina
Quercus agrifolia

Quality: Conscious Assimilation of Experience

Physical Aspects

Coast live oak grows in the valleys and on the slopes of the coastal hills from central to southern California. It forms park-like groves that may seem familiar even if you are not living in California. This is because these groves are often filmed as "the woods scenes" in motion pictures. The Spaniards' name for coast live oak was "encina," which is the evergreen oak of the Mediterranean world.

Coast live oak's leaves are evergreen, small and holly-like, with spiny-toothed edges that are slightly turned under. This oak is known not for its height, but for its habit of spreading out. The tree begins branching out near the base of its deeply furrowed trunk, with very long, horizontal branches. Look for acorns that are one to one-and-one-half inches long, and one-third to one-half covered by a deep cup. This cup has fine, papery scales on the outside, and wood hairs on the inside. These acorns were one of the edible varieties preferred by Native Americans.

Coast Live Oak Deva

You seek a variety of experiences in your life, and the exploration and assimilation of new ideas is a part of your human experience. However, it is possible to inundate yourself with too many experiences at one time, so that you do not learn about the gifts that you are experiencing. I teach you discernment and ask you to first concentrate your focus on the experiences at hand, and integrate them into your being. Then discern which new patterns of energy are for your Highest Good, so that when another person comes to you bearing a gift of awareness, you will be able to understand that gift, and apply it to your own life. When you practice discernment you can focus on what needs to be done with greater clarity, and less waste of your life-force energies.

As you let go of saturating yourself with activities, life will become more relaxing, and pleasurable. Living in the present in this manner will provide you with the openness to welcome new experiences within you, and you will be able to give to others from a purer and more peaceful space.

Spiritual Aspects

Soul Tone: E
Subtle Body Affinities: Emotional/Mental
Element: Air/Earth

Co-creating with Coast Live Oak

The events and activities of your life are your personal garden. If you plant too many flowers or events too close together, they end up competing with each other. Your garden may look under-nourished or cluttered, rather than beautiful and balanced. Coast live oak encourages you to leave enough time and space around an experience for adequate nurturing and cultivation. Then you will more fully appreciate the beauty in your life. If you find yourself valuing "busyness" and trying to cram too many activities into your life, let coast live oak strengthen your ability to see what is really essential. Rather than looking to the future for pleasure and fulfillment, take the time and space to enjoy more fully what is currently present with you.

Affirmation

"I discern what is essential for me to be doing, and I appreciate everything that I do more fully."

EUCALYPTUS

Blue Gum
Eucalyptus globulus

Quality: Increasing Your Physical Vitality

Physical Aspects

Blue gum is the most common variety of eucalyptus in California. Eucalyptus is a native of Australia, which found its way to California, and has spread prolifically in the plains and valleys between the two moutain ranges. It thrives in dry, hot conditions as well as in a variety of other ornamental settings.

Eucalyptus leaves are blue-green, slender and leathery. You may see them turning one edge toward the sun, instead of lying flat, as a way of preserving moisture. The leaves are aromatic when crushed, and are the source of the eucalyptus oil that can clear a stuffy nose. Eucalyptus is considered to be an evergreen, although it drops its leaves at irregular intervals throughout the year. Sunlight filters through the foliage in a way that creates little shade.

The flowers open by shedding a round cap called a calyptus, which is where this family gets its name. When the cap falls off, there are no petals. Instead you see a style and numerous white or red stamens, which spread out like a sunburst. The stamens attract bees, which feed on the plentiful, very sweet nectar. The seeds develop inside a one-inch, black, woody pod.

Eucalyptus Deva

Through my presence you can learn to better monitor
the flow of life-force energy within your physical vehicle.

Sometimes you may not wish to admit that there is a physical imbalance present, because you have a belief that it is in some way weak to be less than perfect, physically. So you ignore the imbalance and hope that it will go away. My energies can travel to an area of an imbalance and signal you that the imbalance is present, so that you can then take action to restore balance. I encourage you to value your physical vehicle.

Your physical vitality is a product of how you breathe. When you breathe shallowly, you are not fully connected to your physical body, or to the emotions that are restricting the flow of life-force energy to your body. You can work with your breath to release any emotions that surround a physical imbalance. Say to yourself, ''I breathe in Light, I breathe out anger, pain, tension.'' When you feel a sense of release and relaxation, continue to breathe in and breathe out Light and Vitality. When you are connected to your physical body, you are able to receive and utilize a greater amount of life-force energy for health and well-being.

Spiritual Aspects

Soul Tone: C#
Subtle Body Affinities: Emotional/Mental
Element: Air

Co-creating with Eucalyptus

Eucalyptus supports you in valuing your physical body and being more aware of its needs. Many of us ignore the message our bodies give us because we do not want to give up a certain lifestyle, or a certain picture of ourselves. We view our bodies as machines that should do as they are told.

In the same way that eucalyptus oil increases the amount of oxygen your physical body receives, the spiritual quality of eucalyptus focuses your attention on your breath as a tool for revitalizing your physical energy. You can work with eucalyptus to deepen your breath, and focus your intent through your breath, on healing a part of your body. As you inhale say, "I breathe in Light (or Love)," and as you exhale, breathe that Light into your physical body. Eucalyptus can heighten your joy in being alive, and feeling good all over.

Affirmation

"I listen to the messages that my physical body is giving me, and I connect with my body through my breath."

VALLEY OAK

California White Oak
Quercus lobata

Quality: Fulfillment

Physical Aspects

Valley oak is the monarch of the deciduous oaks in the West. The tallest white oak on our continent is a valley oak which reigns in state, east of Chico in Butte County. You will find valley oaks in the Sacramento, San Joaquin and Pasadena Valleys, and also in other valleys of central and western California. Valley oak groves are spacious, partly because their roots need lots of room in which to search for water, and because of the way the branches spread out as they grow.

The bark of the old trunks is deeply furrowed, and broken into light gray plates. The leaves with their rounded lobes are very similar in shape to those of the well-known Eastern white oak. In the fall this tree sheds many acorns which look like two-and-one-quarter inch long cartridges. About one third of the nut is enclosed in a round, deep cup with thickened, knobby surfaces.

Valley Oak Deva

The purpose of my energy presence is to help you experience a more complete sense of spiritual fulfillment in your present space. You can take energy from yourself when you seek to move forward in time without honoring the focus, the commitment, and the other inner spiritual resources that have enabled you to fulfill your work. The time for you to feel good about where you are and what you have done is right now.

When you seek to be recognized by your world at large for what you have done, you may feel an instantaneous euphoria that turns out to be short-lived. When its energies have dissipated, a sense of emptiness, or an incompleteness may leave you a little dissatisfied. When you give yourself recognition for what you have accomplished, regardless of the opinions of the outside world, that energy integrates your entire being. The result is that there is a continuity that accompanies you into new experiences beyond the present moment. The stronger you become, the more you affect your own present space, and the space of others around you. When you enjoy what you have completed in the present moment, that joy enhances your being, and you will have truly honored what you have created.

Spiritual Aspects

Soul Tone: F
Subtle Body Affinities: Spiritual
Element: Earth/Air

Co-creating with Valley Oak

Valley oak gives a transcendent resilience that enables you to appreciate the wisdom and beauty that you have created inside yourself through your hard work. Emptiness and feeling that what you do is never quite enough can stem from not honoring your spiritual gains. Valley oak teaches you to enjoy the placement of each stone in your inner foundation, and to value the strength of that foundation.

Affirmation

"My fulfillment comes from honoring the strength and wisdom that I am creating inside me."

INCENSE CEDAR

Calocedrus decurrens

Quality: Purifying the Will

Physical Aspects

Incense cedar is not a true cedar. Rather it is a genus of the cypress family, unlike Western red cedar, which is an arborvitae. Incense cedars are large trees that grow from sixty to one hundred fifty feet tall and three to five feet in diameter. They grow in the mountains from southern Oregon to southern California, and along the lower western slopes of the Sierras, from thirty-five hundred to sixty-five hundred feet in elevation.

If you have never been to the Sierra Nevada mountains before, you might mistake the older growth incense cedars for the giant sequoias. From a distance, the foliage of both trees appears lacy-like, and the bark on both trees is reddish brown and deeply furrowed. However, upon closer inspection, incense cedar leaves are light green, scale-like and flattened, like Western red cedar foliage. Sequoia needles, as we will see later, are pointed and look like little awls.

Incense cedar bark is more cinnamon-colored and stringy, like the bark of other cedars. The prolific cones are oblong and under one inch long, with six pointed cone scales. The name "incense cedar" comes from its fragrant heartwood and aromatic foliage, a special gift of these sturdy trees.

Incense Cedar Deva

I see the foundation for wellness as being the proper use of *will*. There are two aspects to a will that is out of balance. One is where the will is under-utilized in its capacity for action. The second is where the will becomes a weapon, a tool of power and domination over self or others.

When you have difficulty energizing your will, I emphasize that you have every right to be in your present space, deserving that which you desire. The abuse of will leads you into a path of more complex learning experiences, some of which may be painful or disturbing to your system. The process of breaking those patterns is longer and more involved. I teach you to see all sides of the picture so that you can modify your actions to reflect a purity of purpose. Utilized properly, the will is an ally, a positive force in creating wholeness and unity.

Spiritual Aspects

Soul Tone: C#
Subtle Body Affinities: Emotional/Mental
Element: Fire/Earth

Co-creating with Incense Cedar

Like other cedars, incense cedar builds your determination and courage to move through fear, uncertainty and self-doubt so that you can take action. However, incense cedar is especially useful when you want something and feel thwarted or angry when you do not get it. Cedar helps you clarify what your purpose and goals need to be by integrating your individual uniqueness and your spiritual knowing. It can help you divert the strength of your anger into the appropriate channels for action, which is for the Highest Good of all.

Affirmation

"I act according to the Highest Good for all concerned."

CALIFORNIA RED FIR

Shasta Fir
Abies magnifica

Quality: Clearing Subconscious Memories in Adults

Physical Aspects

California red fir is named for its reddish-brown bark, and the reddish tint of the wood. It grows, often in pure stands, from sixty-five hundred feet to nine-thousand feet on the western side of the Sierras, where it is at home with heavy winter snowfalls and dry summers. You will see it at Yosemite, Sequoia, and Kings Canyon National Parks, and around Lake Tahoe. Red fir, like other members of the fir family, displays upright cones rather than cones that hang. Its bark is resinous on the younger trees, and the twigs leave a clean round scar when they are broken off.

Red fir needles are bluish-green and about one inch long, and you twirl them easily between your fingers. The needles grow in two rows along the twig, like grand fir needles.

There is a variety of red fir called Shasta red fir (*Abies magnifica var. shastensis*), which is more prominent around Mt. Shasta, north to Crater Lake in Oregon. Shasta red fir cones have papery bracts extending between the scales, similar to Douglas fir cones. California red fir cones are purplish, with no bracts. Red fir cones from either variety are six to eight inches long. Red fir is a tall tree which sends its heavy crown sixty to one hundred twenty feet high. It truly deserves its Latin name, which means "magnificent."

Red Fir Deva

I can help adult humans to release subconscious energy patterns. Each time you release these patterns you are better prepared to act in the present, and there is less vacillation about what will happen in the future. However, you must make a choice to release a subconscious pattern on all your levels. Do not be afraid to venture into areas of apparent darkness, for it is all part of your growth. Resistance to change is the only thing that keeps you from being your Divine Self.

To release a pattern, first of all you must alleviate the fear of what will happen if you release the memory. I can contribute a sense of detachment and freedom from the pattern. Affirm that you will feel a greater freedom than you have known, upon letting go of this pattern.

You can then ask to return to a time in this life or in a past life where the pattern has surfaced, so that you can see not only its presence, but what effect it had on you in fulfilling your divine purpose at that time. The next step is to affirm with love that the pattern is now disconnected from your energy field. Once again you will have peace with your true nature.

Spiritual Aspects

Soul Tone: A
Subtle Body Affinities: Emotional/Mental
Element: Water/Fire

Co-creating with California Red Fir

Like other members of the fir family, California red fir supports you in bringing painful feelings and beliefs that were repressed due to the lack of tools to deal with them into your conscious awareness. Red fir can aid you in accessing past-life memories, as well as early memories from this present life. If you have difficulty receiving an insight as you are working with red fir, it may help to affirm compassion and self-acceptance, because it is not easy to look at difficult past experiences. You can also focus on what you were to learn from the past experience, and what you need to affirm now. In our experience, all of the firs seem to build a sense of freedom, and a release from burdens that is quite profound.

Affirmation

"I now release past subconscious memories, and I fill my being with Love."

WHITE FIR

Abies concolor

Quality: Clearing Subconscious Memories in Children

Physical Aspects

White fir is a companion tree to red fir, and grows on both the western and eastern slopes of the Sierra Nevadas, in all the National Parks. You will find it at lower elevations than red fir, between three thousand five hundred feet and seven thousand five hundred feet. White fir also grows from southwestern Oregon to Baja California, and in isolated spots in Colorado and New Mexico.

At one-and-one-half to three inches long, its needles are longer than those of red fir, and they have white lines on both the tops and the undersides. The bark on the younger trees is a silvery gray, becoming browner and more deeply furrowed as the tree gets older. Cones, if you can find them, are green or purplish, and three to five inches long.

White Fir Deva

My work is with those of the Human Kingdom who have recently arrived on the Earth Plane—your children. Children have a sensitive and gentle spiritual nature, and I can assist them in maintaining balance as they proceed with their growth on the Earth Plane. I help them to become more immune to any disturbing influences that enter their space. Another function I have is that of clearing subconscious memories. As a concerned adult, you can come with your child to visit me. Encourage your child to sit against me, or hug me, and to share friendship with me. The process of release will happen by itself, and the healing will take place. You can listen actively to the child and encourage him or her to share through your own verbal sharing.

Children's energy patterns are more flexible, and their openness and Unconditional Love creates the receptivity in their emotional and mental bodies for healing.

Spiritual Aspects

Soul Tone: A
Subtle Body Affinities: Emotional/Mental
Element: Water/Fire

Co-creating with White Fir

White fir energy seems gentler and "less dense" than red fir energy. White fir works with children because their subconscious memories are more accessible, and they respond to its delicate and protective nature. The story of "Jennifer and the Little Fir" was inspired by this tree, with the thought that parents might share it with their children.

Affirmation

"White fir, you are my special friend."

SUGAR PINE

Pinus lambertiana

Quality: Emotional Empathy

Physical Aspects

Sugar pine is the largest, and probably the most magnificent of the world's one hundred species of pines. The old growth trees are commonly six feet thick and over two hundred feet tall. Sugar pine's long, spreading branches stand out at right angles to the trunk, forming a broad, flat crown that contrasts with the sharp spires of other conifers. Its bluish-green needles are two to four inches long and grouped in bunches of five. The rough bark is generally gray to reddish-brown, with smaller plates, and shallower furrows than those of ponderosa pine bark.

Sugar pine has the largest cones of any North American conifer. These cones are one foot to twenty inches long and weigh up to four pounds. During their second summer, the female seed-bearing cones release their seeds, which are highly prized by birds and squirrels.

Sugar pine is named for the sweet globules of resin which come from the bark when it is injured. It grows from southwestern Oregon to Baja California. South of Alpine County, sugar pine grows on the western slope of the Sierras, between forty-five hundred feet and seventy-five hundred feet in elevation. It is easily seen at Yosemite National Park.

Sugar Pine Deva

In your society you have been taught to view life as a state of polarized opposites. You have to be right or wrong, good or bad, winner or loser. When you paint a picture of an experience in black and white only, your process of learning becomes totally shut down, and you condemn yourself. You can learn to go beyond viewing experiences in terms of all good or all bad, or winning and losing, by developing the quality of *emotional empathy*.

I develop your emotional empathy of self, for self. When you criticize yourself, you turn your emotional nature against yourself, ultimately restricting your responses to an experience. Empathy is being able to identify emotionally with any experience in a constructive manner. Your emotional nature then becomes an active catalyst in energizing a more spontaneous approach to the situation.

When you find yourself in a frustrating experience, you can berate yourself for having entered the experience. Or you can look for the underlying energies which can strengthen you emotionally, so that you have a more affirmative sense of self, and clarity in your direction.

It is possible to release an experience and bring yourself into a more neutral state of being regarding the situation. When you add the quality of emotional empathy, you revitalize yourself with greater understanding to meet new experiences. You are willing to try again. Your approach to living becomes more lighthearted because you experience life from a broader point of view. Remember this: it is through learning and experience that knowledge is gained. Knowledge leads to wisdom, and wisdom is priceless.

Spiritual Aspects

Soul Tone: C
Subtle Body Affinities: Emotional/Mental
Element: Fire

Co-creating with Sugar Pine

Moving beyond self-judgment is the special gift of the pine family. Sugar pine strengthens your emotional ability to validate your actions. When you take an action that later seems like a mistake, you always have a reason that makes sense on the emotional level. To better understand what is happening to you emotionally, try relaxing yourself and then call on the child inside of you. Ask what the child wants emotionally in the situation, and give this quality to your inner child. You will find that self-blame dissolves into emotional acceptance and understanding. There is a lighthearted, playful quality about sugar pine that encourages you to send your inner child into the sunlight.

Affirmation
"I accept the needs of my inner child."

JEFFREY PINE
Pinus jeffreyi

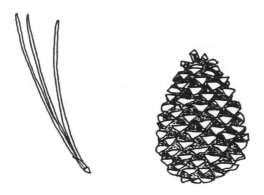

Quality: Versatility

Physical Aspects

Jeffrey pine grows mainly in the Sierra Nevadas from six thousand to nine thousand feet, and is quite common at Lake Tahoe. The bark gives off a wonderful pineapple-vanilla fragrance that scents the surrounding woods. The bark of Jeffrey pine is darker and appears more furrowed than sugar or ponderosa pine bark.

Like ponderosa pine needles, Jeffrey pine needles are about ten inches long and grouped in bundles of three. However, its cones are larger, about six or seven inches long and the spines on the scales point down, so that you can pick up this cone without discomfort. Ponderosa cones are smaller and more prickly. Jeffrey pine, with its delicious scent and smooth cones, is altogether a friendly tree.

Jeffrey Pine Deva

It is a common human practice to set personal expectations, in order to encourage movement toward a particular goal. However, sometimes you discover that your personal expectations may not reflect all that you need to learn, in order to accomplish your ultimate goal. You may need to make unexpected but necessary changes along your chosen path. Then you may have a tendency to blame yourself for not being more foresighted, or for being different than you wanted to be.

My energies help you to mentally expand your definition of the standard by which you are operating, so that you can take a more compassionate view of where you stand. I help you to mentally sense the dichotomy between the former direction and the new direction, so that you have a greater mental understanding of the process of growth that you have undertaken. You will then find many more alternatives to explore as part of the fulfillment of your goal. Above all, I help you to open your mind to greater acceptance of your own space, wherever you happen to be.

Spiritual Aspects

Soul Tone: C
Subtle Body Affinities: Mental, Spiritual
Element: Fire

Co-creating with Jeffrey Pine

Jeffrey pine aids you in releasing self-criticism, by strengthening your mental capacity to see how you limit yourself in setting goals that are too narrow in scope. So many times our goals are based on conclusions drawn by comparing ourselves with others, and Jeffrey pine, like other pines, builds compassion and self-acceptance for who you are in the moment. Jeffrey pine supports your release of the pain of believing that there is only one way to accomplish a given goal. It encourages a versatility in thinking, and a flexibility of approach, where you affirm who you are in any situation. Jeffrey pine also connects you with your spiritual knowing so that you can see how apparent detours are in reality part of your main path.

Affirmation

"I am following my direction with a versatile tolerance that affirms who I am in the present moment."

GIANT SEQUOIA

Big Tree, Sierra Redwood
Sequoiadendron giganteum

Quality: The Mastery of Transcendence

Physical Aspects

The experience of the giant sequoia cannot be described in words; you simply have to go to the narrow strip of the Sierra Nevadas where they grow. The most famous groves are the Mariposa Grove at Yosemite National Park, and several groves in Sequoia National Park. They can be found between five thousand and seven thousand feet in elevation.

Sequoias are immense. The old growth trees *average* ten to fifteen feet in diameter and about two hundred fifty feet in height. The first limb of General Sherman, the largest tree, would stretch out over a twelve-story office building. This limb is seven feet thick and one hundred twenty-five feet long—a tree in itself.

The largest sequoias are over twenty-two hundred years old and may be as old as thirty-two hundred years. They are highly resistant to death by fire because of their thick bark, and the tannin present in the wood. Tannin is a substance that is used in fire extinguishers. It is assumed that an old tree has been subjected to fire not less than every twenty-five years. Thus a tree that is three thousand years old has been subjected to a hundred or more fires. Sequoia wood is also decay-, disease- and insect-resistant.

Seguoias do not begin to produce a quantity of cones until they are about two centuries old. The female, seed-producing cones mature in their second year when they are about the size and shape of a chicken egg. The seeds inside the cones are spread by squirrels who love the fleshy scales of the cones, but not the tiny seeds.

The needles of the sequoia are unlike the needles of any other conifer. They are blue-green, pointed, and look like little awls that are about one-quarter inch long. It has been said, and we agree, that the coastal redwood has a more "feminine grace," while the giant sequoia has a more "masculine majesty." It is fortunate that most of these rare trees are now protected.

Giant Sequoia Deva

When you look upon me with awe and see the magnitude of my physical structure, I can unite you with your spiritual self. When you are attuned to your spiritual nature, you can then function in the state of transcendence. Transcendence means being able to understand beyond what is apparent on the surface, and to respond in a far more encompasing manner. Living in the state of transcendence therefore has a powerful impact on the way that you understand the realities of life, and what others can learn from you.

Transcendence means learning that you can overcome any experience no matter how devastating. When I am confronted with the experience of a forest fire, I see it in its natural state as promoting growth and change. When someone from the Human Kingdom is responsible for that fire, I respond to that being with compassion and Unconditional Love. This is because any judgment of this particular being would only deepen the pattern that resulted in its manifestation as fire. I accept what takes place within Nature as being part of a larger cycle. When change occurs, there are always the signs of renewal. Be open to this renewal, and know that change contributes to your maturity as a being.

Transcendence is knowing that life does not end. As you grow, you will learn to be gentle and compassionate, and to give without feeling the need to receive. You will also learn the meaning of creativity and abundance. You will be living in total Oneness with the Infinite.

Spiritual Aspects

Soul Tone: High C
Subtle Body Affinities: Spiritual, Emotional/Mental
Element: Fire

Co-creating with Giant Sequoia

Experiencing the giant sequoia is like listening to the triumphant music of Beethoven's "Symphony # 9" or Handel's "Messiah." In times of tragedy, when part of you dies, giant sequoia shows you that only an outer manifestation has changed. Your will to live survives, and grows again in the spring of new beginnings. Your strength becomes invincible, and your endurance becomes part of the Light that creates a new you that was only a seed before.

Affirmation

"The Unconditional Love of God transcends all human conditions and experiences."

11 | Trees of the Rocky Mountains

MORE THAN A HUNDRED north-south ranges make up the Rocky Mountains, which stretch from Alaska to Mexico, like a long backbone. These mountain ranges reach their greatest width in Colorado and Utah. The mountains north of Yellowstone National Park are generally considered the Northern Rockies. Here you will find Western red cedar, Western hemlock and grand fir, trees that were discussed earlier in the chapter on Pacific Northwest trees.

The Southern Rockies consist of long, uplifted ridges with upturned foothills on either side. Douglas fir, also discussed in the Northwest chapter, makes its appearance here as a smaller tree among the giant pines. In this chapter we will describe the prominent trees that we saw in Rocky Mountain National Park.

LODGEPOLE PINE

Tamarack Pine
Pinus contorta (var. latifolia)

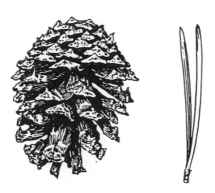

Quality: Resilience

Physical Aspects

Lodgepole pine comes in three distinct varieties. The shore pine (*var. contorta*) is a small, twisted tree that grows along the Pacific coast from southeastern Alaska to northern California. The Sierra lodgepole (*var. murrayana*) loves the Sierra Nevada high country between sixty-five hundred feet and ten thousand five hundred feet. It can grow up to three feet thick. We will discuss the Rocky Mountain lodgepole, which is prominent in the Cascades, and the Northern and Southern Rockies.

For the novice tree buff, lodgepole pine is easy to identify because it is the only local pine with needles in bunches of two. The needles themselves are about two inches long, stout, and sometimes twisted. The bark is grayish-brown and scaly, and divided by cracks. Lodgepole pine cones are the smallest Western pine cones, about one to two inches long, and prickly. Often they will tenaciously hang on the trees for decades.

Lodgepole pine depends on fire for its renewal, because it is a sun-loving species that gets shaded out by firs and other shade-tolerant trees. Lodgepole pine cones only open when they are heated by a forest fire, and then the pines re-seed quickly to become the pioneer trees of the fire site.

Lodgepole Pine Deva

When you find yourself at an apparent standstill in life, you may feel that you have lost connection with the particular process in which you are engaged. I tell you that there can be flow even when it appears that no movement is taking place. There are times when inner work is necessary for rest, for evaluation, and for reassessment of your process. My energies can help you clear doubt and self-judgment when you are in this space of inner movement rather than outer movement.

If you find yourself feeling worthless because you have lost faith in your process, I strengthen your belief in yourself so that you can let go of self-criticism. When you judge yourself as worthless, you diminish your sense of purpose in living. My energies can help you to stop drifting so that you can evaluate where you are and what you need to be doing. I encourage you to keep trying even when the steps seem so small and the journey endless. Value your times of inner work as well as your times of outward movement. Release the self-criticism that says that you must be moving forward with something tangible to show for your work. I ask you to hold the vision of my cones opening to release the seeds that usher in the beginning of new life. Your seeds germinate through your belief in yourself.

Spiritual Aspects

Soul Tone: C
Subtle Body Affinities: Emotional/Mental
Element: Fire

Co-creating with Lodgepole Pine

Like other pines, lodgepole pine helps you to release self-judgment. If self-blame and feelings of worthlessness have led to despondency, despair and a loss of goal direction, then lodgepole pine can motivate you to begin again. It provides a sense of valuing self that feels like a stabilizing inner core of certainty. Its energy is also dependable and tenacious, like a rock that you climb onto to get your bearings, when you feel caught in a raging stream. As you set off again, you are stronger, more durable, and more focused on your course.

Affirmation

"I tenaciously hold to my path, reassured that I am closer to Greater Light."

PONDEROSA PINE

Western Yellow Pine
Pinus ponderosa

Quality: Forgiveness

Physical Aspects

You can find ponderosa pine on sunny mountainsides in every Western state. You will see it on the eastern side of the Cascades and other inland ranges in Washington and Oregon. It is a companion to Jeffrey and sugar pine in the Sierras in California. Ponderosa pine ranges south to northern Mexico and as far east as the Black Hills of South Dakota. We describe ponderosa pine in this chapter because it is one of the dominant trees of the Southern Rockies at lower elevations, along with lodgepole pine.

The name "ponderosa" comes from "ponderous," which expressed botanical explorer David Douglas's opinion of the size of this tree. Ponderosa pine is generally easy to identify because of several striking features. Its bark exhibits large, smooth, cinnamon-red plates, and pieces that break off are yellow inside. The long, six- to ten-inch needles generally come in bunches of three. Cones are two to six inches long and prickly to the touch.

Ponderosa Pine Deva

The lesson of forgiveness of self and others is one of the more difficult lessons to learn on the earth plane. You have found it hard to love those who have contributed energy to your own thoughts of unworthiness. When you have accepted the need for forgiveness, I give a serenity of mind that allows you to enter a space that is devoid of judgment. In this space you are accepted for the Light Being that you are. When you can allow yourself to be loved, you can begin the process of releasing unworthiness. You can also look at the source of the pattern of unworthiness, and understand how it unfolded the way it did in your life. Forgiveness also manifests when there is a recognition of the imperfection that is part of living in a physical reality. You do not need to carry the excess burden of trying to be infallible. You are learning to accept where you are, and to be at peace with the experiences that you have chosen for soul growth. When you can forgive, you open the doorway to deeper connections with others. You can look into the mirror of life and see your true nature expressed in the fulfillment of your divine purpose.

Spiritual Aspects

Soul Tone: C
Subtle Body Affinities: Emotional, Spiritual
Element: Fire/Water

Co-creating with Ponderosa Pine

The ultimate gift of the pine family is releasing self-criticism through forgiveness. Ponderosa pine works profoundly when you have been holding a grudge against another, or if you have been unable to forgive yourself. It calms you so that you can tap your spiritual knowingness in times of intensity. Ponderosa pine strengthens your compassion for yourself, and asks you to forgive your imperfections. This pine lets you know that you can be a human with faults, and a divinely beloved being at the same time. Ponderosa pine also helps with long-standing beliefs about who you feel you need to be or what you think you need to accomplish.

Affirmation

"I accept myself as I am, and I forgive myself and others."

BLUE SPRUCE

Colorado Spruce
Picea pungens

Quality: Peace

Physical Aspects

Blue spruce is the state tree of Colorado and is most prominent near canyon streamsides in Colorado and the central Rockies. You will see it at elevations from six thousand to ten thousand feet. You have probably noticed blue spruce planted as an ornamental, because it is famous for the silvery-blue tinge of its needles. Like other spruces, these needles are four-sided and sharp, and they grow one-half to one inch long. Blue spruce bark seems to be a grayer brown than Engelmann spruce bark, and blue spruce cones are nearly twice as long.

Blue Spruce Deva

I tell you to fulfill your spiritual purpose by demonstrating to others the quality of peace in everything that you do. Being at peace is feeling fulfilled with what you have accomplished. You fulfill yourself by honoring your own individuality in each step that is required for the process of creation. You find peace when you take time to appreciate rather than judge that which you have brought into manifestation.

There are times when what you have created falls short, when viewed from the perspective of the outer world. It is then that my energies tell you to look not only at the finished product, but at what you have truly gained in the process of creation itself. It is not always what is created that is significant, but rather, what you have become in the process. When you are working with peace as your foundation, time itself is no longer perceived as a restriction. As you honor your internal rhythms, you will find that peace unfolds within you in a state of harmony and balance.

Spiritual Aspects

Soul Tone: C
Subtle Body Affinities: Spiritual
Element: Fire/Earth

Co-creating with Blue Spruce

Blue spruce energy is light and joyful, as well as peaceful. It seems in some ways to express the culmination of the journey to find and manifest your spiritual purpose. It is the understanding that right action involves both embracing your physical reality with greater stewardship, and becoming a mirror of love and peace for others. Every action comes from a centered and balanced core of Unconditional Love. Blue spruce is helpful if you feel a lack of fulfillment in what you are accomplishing, or if your tendency is to focus on the end product rather than the process of your spiritual awakening.

Affirmation

"Everything that I share with others is born from the Inner Peace within me."

ENGELMANN SPRUCE

Mountain Spruce
Picea engelmanni

Quality: Wisdom

Physical Aspects

Engelmann spruce is native to the high Rockies from Canada to Arizona, from three thousand feet in the north, to twelve thousand feet in the south. It is often found with lodgepole pine and subalpine fir, on cool moist slopes. We also found it with blue spruce in Rocky Mountain National Park. Engelmann spruce needles are dark green, four-sided, and about one inch long. You will find them sharp and stiff to the touch. The bark is russet red, and broken into thin, loosely attached scales. Cones are brown, cylindrical, and one-and-one-half to two-and-one-half inches long. Compared with the giant pines, this tree is medium-sized and more compact, but nevertheless picturesque.

One way to tell a spruce from a fir is to gently pull a needle from its twig. A fir needle will leave a round, flat scar. A spruce needle is attached to a small peg, which makes a spruce twig very bumpy. When you pull off a spruce needle, the peg will remain, or the needle will carry a small splinter at its base.

Engelmann Spruce Deva

My energies help you to understand the importance of uniting your mental and emotional nature, in your expression of your spiritual purpose. When your emotional nature is not connected with your spiritual path, there may be a sense of incompleteness, or a dedication without joy. You may have learned from the past of the volatility and rapid change that the emotions can bring to your state of being. I help you to view your emotional nature in a more compassionate manner, to see your feelings as a positive expression of who you are, rather than a source of turmoil or instability.

Your emotional nature is a vehicle to express the Consciousness of Spirit through your unique purpose in being. When you are living spiritually through your emotional body, the judgment, anger and fear cannot exist within you. I can support you in healing emotional pain that you have experienced from the past, by helping you develop a greater empathy and compassion for self. Your emotional nature teaches you to transfer that empathy to others. To learn about your emotional nature takes patience, and persistence. When you fulfill your spiritual purpose through uniting your mental and emotional natures, you become a far greater empathic light. As you reflect this focused light, joy lives and breathes throughout your being.

Spiritual Aspects

Soul Tone: C
Subtle Body Affinities: Emotional/Mental, Spiritual
Element: Fire/Earth

Co-creating with Engelmann Spruce

The spruce family strengthens your commitment to your spiritual purpose and its fullest expression. There comes a time in your spiritual growth when you need to reclaim your connection to your feelings, and to heal the emotional wounds that diminish your fullest expression of who you are. Engelmann spruce encourages you to honor the emotional part of your being and to heal emotional numbness and insensitivity. Engelmann spruce increases your capacity for deeper joy and appreciation for self and others, which are steps leading to wisdom. Your whole being hums with aliveness when you open to this tree.

Affirmation

"I am now expressing my spiritual essence on all levels of my being."

QUAKING ASPEN

Trembling Poplar
Populus tremuloides

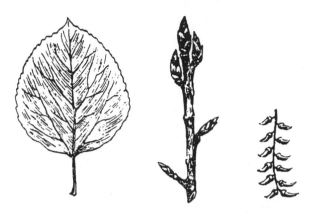

Quality: Moving from Anxiety to Opportunity

Physical Aspects

Quaking aspen is a member of the poplar family, which also includes the cottonwoods. It is the most widely distributed broadleaf tree in North America. You will find it scattered across the northern section of our country, and throughout the Western mountains south to California and Arizona. When you think of Rocky Mountain trees, you probably think of quaking aspens, basking on gravelly hillsides and sparkling yellow in the autumn sunlight.

A Native American name for this tree is "noisy leaf," because of the way its leaves flutter on their soft, flexible stems. The olive green to white tones on aspen bark are also eye-catching. The heart-shaped leaves of the quaking aspen are small and almost round.

Quaking aspen trees are either male or female, and in April their catkins are different colors, depending on the sex of the tree. Quaking aspen is another tree like lodgepole pine, that cheerfully germinates on burned sites, and provides shade for the larger trees to grow.

Quaking Aspen Deva

When the flow of life-force energies has become constricted from fear, then you may have difficulty maintaining the focus and intensity needed to move through your experiences. By showing you additional facets to the process that you may not have seen, I stimulate you to take that next step. I can help paint a picture of the process that is more dynamic, so that you can connect more enthusiastically and completely with it.

My energies are helpful in sustaining you during difficult times as you commit yourself to moving forward with your chosen task. When you continue through an experience even when you have fear, you enhance your own inner strength. You also expand your perspective on the choices available to you.

Spiritual Aspects

Soul Tone: G
Subtle Body Affinities: Emotional/Mental
Element: Air/Earth

Co-creating with Quaking Aspen

Aspens can give a sense of safety, an anchoring in times of change. It becomes easier to affirm that everything is going to be all right. When you feel like the bottom has dropped out from under you, or you are troubled with anxiety and fear about an upcoming experience, quaking aspen restores your sense of perspective. When you see more possibilities for learning and growth, then it is easier to move with a sense of anticipation. The leaves of the aspen enjoy the wind from all sides, and they speak of the exuberance of living life fully in the face of challenge.

Affirmation

"Fear becomes an opportunity, as I affirm safety in opening to new possibilities for growth."

12 | Trees of the Midwest

ONCE YOU LEAVE the Rockies and head east, the clumps of trees around homesteads become oases in a vast panorama of sky and brown hills. The rebirth of the forest in the midsection of our country comes as a welcome feast for tree lovers.

This chapter describes some prominent Middle Western trees that we visited while in Nebraska, Iowa and Indiana. Except for box elder, these species are more local to this region. Box elder has a wider range, which includes the East as well. The five deciduous trees in this chapter are arranged alphabetically according to their species.

The Middle West is a melting pot for trees from other areas of the country. From the West you will find quaking aspen and cotton-wood, a variety of which we will discuss in this chapter. Although white pine is given with the Eastern evergreens, some of its best stands are found in Minnesota, Wisconsin and Michigan. Those of you from the East will recognize your old friends white oak, hickory, maple, sycamore, beech, tulip tree and willow. Trees that are common from the South include black walnut and sweetgum.

All of these trees are able to withstand variations in temperature, and periods of dry weather that are common to the Middle West. Perhaps we value them even more because we cannot take them for granted. They seem to stand in strength by themselves, connecting the open spaces of earth with the sky.

BOX ELDER

Ashleaf Maple
Acer negundo

Quality: Spiritual Expansion

Physical Aspects

Box elder can be found in all states east of the Great Plains, but it is especially common in the moist, fertile soils of the Middle West. It is classified botanically as a maple because of its two-winged seeds that hang on the tree most of the winter. However, although this tree has some physical characteristics like maple and ash, it is truly a unique species in and of itself.

Box elder leaves are compound, like ash leaves. The three to five leaflets (usually three) vary in shape, and they look like poison ivy leaves.

If you touch the glossy twigs, a white coating may rub off on your fingers. For classification in winter, look for narrow leaf scars that meet in raised points on opposite sides of the twigs. This tree has a hardiness that lies underneath its relatively unassuming presence.

Box Elder Deva

While on the earth, you become more dependent on the use of your emotional and mental energies in working with experiences in life. This is only natural because it is part of your learning process. However, the use of your mental and emotional energies gives you only one aspect of reality. I can help you clarify an experience more clearly from a spiritual perspective, by removing the clutter of conflicting feelings and thoughts, so that only the spiritual meaning or teaching from the experience remains. You will then be able to receive more positive life-force energy from the situation, and assimilate that which is for your Highest Good. As you reintegrate more fully your spiritual wisdom into your everyday actions, you will bring greater happiness and peace into your life.

Spiritual Aspects

Soul Tone: A
Subtle Body Affinities: Spiritual, Emotional/Mental
Element: Air

Co-creating with Box Elder

Box elder is a wonderful tree with which to deepen your meditative skills. It aids you in stilling your mind, and puts you in touch with your Higher Guidance, in order to bring into focus the broader meaning of an experience. Box elder affirms the joy of being One With All Life. Its energy is gentle and very uplifting, and can ease any fear that you may have about connecting with your spiritual nature.

Affirmation

"I open to my spiritual nature, in order to seek that which is for my Highest Good."

OHIO BUCKEYE

Aesculus glabra

Quality: Learning and Letting Go

Physical Aspects

Ohio Buckeye is a smaller native American relation to the European horsechestnut (*Aesculus hippocastum*), which is widely planted in this country as an ornamental. The Ohio buckeye grows in moist woods from Ohio to northern Alabama, and west into eastern Kansas and Oklahoma.

The compound leaf consists of five leaflets that are each three to six inches long, which fan out from a central point. It bears big, yellow flowers in the spring, and the leaves turn a bright yellow in the fall.

The shell of a buckeye nut is covered with sharp warts. The nut itself has a white patch on its base that is said to look like the eye of a deer, hence the name "buckeye." If you break a dead twig, a fallen buckeye leaf, or a piece of discarded bark, you will notice a distinctive odor, which also identifies this tree.

Ohio Buckeye Deva

When the outcome of an experience is not what you desired, you may find yourself questioning the meaning of that experience, and worrying about the overall effects of the experience on future actions. You may ask over and over, "What if I had done this instead?" Self-doubt and worry about the opinions of others may keep you reliving the experience, rather than learning from it and going on.

I help you to find the positive learning from a difficult experience so that you can clear it from your thoughts. I also support you in releasing patterns of self-doubt that you may create in response to criticism from others. Through my energies you can better discern whether someone else's words need your consideration, or whether they represent that person's own insecurities. I can show you pictures of how others perceive you, and what your true nature really is. When you re-create the safety of a well-defined personal space, you can then let go of an outcome which is not what you expected, and the true you becomes stronger and more able to handle diverse experiences.

Spiritual Aspects

Soul Tone: A
Subtle Body Affinities: Emotional/Mental
Element: Water/Fire

Co-creating with Ohio Buckeye

The horsechesnut family (*Aesculus*) helps you learn from difficult experiences and then let them go. Ohio Buckeye is a "self-esteem strengthener" when you have let self-doubt about an experience contribute to a lack of assertiveness, oversensitivity to criticism, or difficulty in putting things in perspective. When you have a tendency to replay the drama like a broken record, Ohio buckeye reminds you to believe in yourself and not let mistakes or the opinions of others get you down. Then you are better able to see an experience for what it is and let it go. Ohio buckeye can help you with a specific experience that has had a difficult outcome, or when you have chosen a path in life that others may disagree with through lack of understanding. Its quality of positive affirmation cheers you on to take events in your stride with your sense of self intact, and without looking back.

Affirmation

"I learn from an experience through believing in myself and not looking back."

EASTERN COTTONWOOD

Eastern Poplar
Populus deltoides

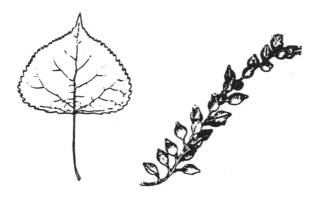

Quality: Honoring Your Physical Body

Physical Aspects

Eastern cottonwood grows close to streams and moist places from Quebec to the foothills of the Rockies, and south to Texas. The leathery leaves of this tree are triangular, with coarse, right-angled teeth and a wide mid-vein. If you find this tree in winter, you can gently pick off a bud on the end of a fallen twig, and you will find that it sticks to your fingers. Like black cottonwood, Eastern cottonwood blankets the ground in late spring with white, cottony seeds, like a soft snowfall. Eastern cottonwood is very resilient, taking in its stride the heavy winds, drought, hot summers and cold winters of the Great Plains.

Eastern Cottonwood Deva

I help you to change your beliefs about self that are present within your physical vehicle. When you function in a state of fear or anxiety, you disconnect yourself from your physical vehicle. Becoming attuned to your spiritual nature means recognizing the importance of honoring your physical vehicle. You learn to be more aware of resting when you need it, and providing nourishment that adds to your life force energy. ''Physical fitness'' does not mean ''over-extension.'' Rather, it means moving with moderation, stability, and balance. The more empathic you are toward your physical vehicle, the more harmony you create within your being. The natural cycles of Nature can teach you about the continuity and the integration of growth. The Unconditional Love present in Nature can teach you to love your physical form and to let go of self-judgment. My affirmation to you is to center in the present moment, for that is where you find joy in being with your physical vehicle.

Spiritual Aspects

Soul Tone: C
Subtle Body Affinities: Emotional/Mental
Element: Water/Earth

Co-creating with Eastern Cottonwood

The cottonwoods help you to remember that your physical body is a sacred temple that needs to be honored. Eastern cottonwood calls attention to your physical needs, when you have decided that your body will just have to go along with whatever you are desiring at the moment. With Eastern cottonwood, you can learn to see your body as more than a machine that you order around. Its energy supports you in learning the patience and acceptance that is the foundation for a more intuitively complete connection with your physical body.

Affirmation

"I live harmoniously within self by honoring my body, mind and spirit."

SHELLBARK HICKORY

Carya laciniosa

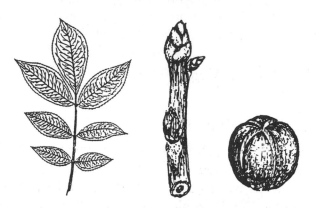

Quality: Mental Focus

Physical Aspects

Shellbark hickory is the tough, Midwestern relative of the Eastern shagbark hickory. It is found west of the Allegheny Mountains, and often with mossycup oak and white oak. Shellbark hickory is easy to identify because of its shaggy, gray bark that seems to hang in loose strips. The bark does not begin to shag, however, until it is around forty years old, when the tree begins to bear nuts.

Shellbark hickory leaves are compound, and each leaf has seven leaflets that are hairy beneath, with fine-toothed margins. The leaflets are each from four to seven inches long, with the three biggest leaves at the tip. In the winter, look for stout, hairy twigs with very large end buds and prominent, orange-colored leaf scars. Squirrels prize these hickory nuts which are about two inches long. Their thick husks split into four pieces when ripe.

Shellbark Hickory Deva

My energies strengthen your capacity to separate the essential from the non-essential thoughts so that you can give full attention to the completion of the task at hand. I help you to organize and prioritize your thoughts, so that you can proceed logically through your task. Sometimes when you act impulsively and scatter your energies or try to skip steps, you are led off course. You may ultimately become disillusioned and have great difficulty in completing your goal. When your attention is focused and your steps are logical, you will have both the concentration and the reserves of energy that you need to remain balanced.

Spiritual Aspects

Soul Tone: G
Subtle Body Affinities: Mental
Element: Air/Earth

Co-creating with Shellbark Hickory

Like a river current, shellbark hickory energy gently keeps you on course with a task, when you have a tendency to act impulsively, and get carried away by an eddy of excitement into a sidepool. Shellbark hickory helps you discriminate which ideas need priority. It also assists you in keeping in mind the broader perspective of what you want to accomplish. When you feel scattered by various demands on your attention, shellbark hickory energy balances your mind with a calm blend of both focus and perspective.

Affirmation

"I prioritize my thoughts, in order to maintain my focus and complete my tasks."

MOSSYCUP OAK

Bur Oak
Quercus macrocarpa

Quality: Continuity Through Integration

Physical Aspects

Mossycup oak or bur oak is the "white oak" of the Middle West. It also grows as far south as Arkansas and Texas, and as far west as Montana. Mossycup oak endures smoke and city smog to give beauty and shade to Chicago and other Mid-Western cities.

Mossycup oak is unique because of its large, six- to twelve-inch leaves. These leaves have the rounded tips of the white oak group, and in addition, they are almost divided in two by at least one deep pair of indentations of the leaf lobes. You can be even more certain that you have found mossycup oak if you notice lots of deep, bowl-shaped acorn cups with heavy spines on the rim. Mossycup oak bark is light gray and generally shallow-grooved. This is a tree that you can rely on, and it adds a stability and sturdiness to the woods and parks where it is found.

Mossycup Oak Deva

Every growth process has a beginning and a completion. What brings continuity to the growth process is assessing what has been learned, and planning the next steps. When you don't know where to go next, I activate your mental resources so that you understand the link that runs from where you are to where you are going in the next moment. When you honor the gifts that you have present with you in your life, you can then see the underlying purpose of a particular process. I encourage you to recognize how you can use your talents and skills in new and expanding ways, to clarify your next steps. Release your expectations of how your process will ultimately manifest, so that you can affirm that your creation is where it needs to be in the process itself.

Once your conceptual picture is clear, then you can engage the energy of your emotional desires to bring about the result that you are seeking. When you affirm a goal with feeling behind it, the interweaving of your mental and emotional energy becomes the springboard for your new expression.

Spiritual Aspects

Soul Tone: F
Subtle Body Affinities: Mental, Emotional
Element: Earth/Air

Co-creating with Mossycup Oak

Mossycup oak renews your sense of continuity by affirming the rightness of what you are doing. Fear and hesitation can contribute to a sense of confusion about your next steps, so that your actions may seem isolated. Like other members of the oak family, mossycup oak heightens your awareness of your resources, so that you can proceed with the strength that comes from your inner center. In addition, mossycup oak facilitates the mental evaluation and planning of where you are going, and how you are going to get there. When you can integrate your personal resources with what you are learning and your sense of purpose, you create stability for yourself, as well as a continuity in your flow.

Affirmation

"I integrate my personal resources in order to provide continuity between my present and future actions."

13 | Eastern Evergreens

THE "GREAT AMERICAN WOODS" of the East stretch roughly from the Mississippi River to the Atlantic and Gulf coasts. Except in the North, these are predominantly broadleaf trees of infinite variety, with distinct, colorful seasons.

We begin with the Eastern evergreens, which predominate in the Great Lakes region, New England, and the higher elevations of the Appalachian Mountains. However, you will find them everywhere in the East, with their pungent fragrance and dark, mysterious shade. They are smaller than their Western counterparts, but similar in their physical appearance, so that they are easily recognized. The evergreens in this chapter are conifers, and keep their needles all year, except for bald cypress.

BALD CYPRESS

Swamp Cypress
Taxodium distichum

Quality: Outer and Inner Security

Physical Aspects

Often festooned with Spanish moss, bald cypress graces the southern swamps and streambanks of the Atlantic coastal plain from Maryland to Florida, and westward to Texas. However, it grows well on land also and has been extensively planted for this reason. Like the larch family, the bald cypress is another conifer whose needles turn yellow or orange and drop in the autumn along with their twigs. In winter, without its needles or twigs, this tree can appear to be dead.

Bald cypress needles are pale green, fairly flat, and feathery in appearance. Many people know bald cypress as the tree with the "knees." These knees are roots that project up out of the swamp water to get air for the tree. The trunk flares out at the base like the shoulder of a bottle, and the bark is gray to reddish-brown, stringy and coarse.

Bald cypress bears a one-inch, brown cone, which matures in one season. Under the thick scales are the seeds, which spread by floating, to root in the mud. Bald cypress is also known for its extremely durable wood.

Bald Cypress Deva

There have been times when you have felt insecure and worried about the lack of monetary resources, or meaningful relationships in your life. I tell you that you give away your personal power when you search outside yourself for a sense of security. Insecurity has its roots in self-judgment, feelings of inadequacy, and a lack of Unconditional Love for self. I convey to you that your inner resources are your support. You do indeed have within you the confidence that you are seeking, the ability to think clearly and decisively, and the expanded understanding of your spiritual resources. Instead of acquiring money or seeking recognition as a way to feel secure, acknowledge within you your own strength. When you do this you build greater independence and self-reliance. You can release the fear of errors in judgment by understanding that you are always learning, and that is a gain. My energies confirm to you that you have the resources you need inside you, in order to live with a sense of safety and abundance, rather than insecurity and lack.

Spiritual Aspects

Soul Tone: C
Subtle Body Affinities: Emotional/Mental
Element: Fire

Co-creating with Bald Cypress

Bald cypress addresses the issue of "If I only had this amount of dollars, that particular job, a special relationship, etc., I would be happy." It is the issue of looking to the lives of others, or things outside yourself, to bring fulfillment. If you are feeling empty, insecure or worried about the lack in your life, bald cypress directs your awareness to your own strengths. It also has a kind of cathartic quality which can direct your focus inward when you are seeking "goodies" in the form of love from the world. Bald cypress affirms your self-reliance and self-confidence, so that you are ready to move forward in the security of your own power.

Affirmation

"I am centered in the security and abundance of my own power."

EASTERN RED CEDAR

Red juniper
juniperus virginiana

Quality: Courage

Physical Aspects

Eastern red cedar thrives in old fields as well as forests throughout the East, and the Middle West. This is also the cedar that is known for its beautiful, aromatic wood. The French Canadians called this cedar "baton rouge" meaning "red stick." When they found this tree in Louisiana, they named their capital after it.

You will usually find two types of needles on a red cedar tree. One type is three-sided, sharp and prickly. The other needles are scale-like, and compressed to form a four-sided branchlet.

Another good way to distinguish Eastern red cedar from other cedars is by its hard, sky-blue berries, which are the characteristic fruits of the juniper family.

You may also see an orange or brown "cedar gall" resting on the needles after heavy rains. This is the fungus apple rust, which lives on cedars during the second half of its life cycle. These galls dry up in dry weather.

Eastern Red Cedar Deva

When you are seeking to have your personal will more reflective of your Divine Will, it is essential at times for you to step into experiences even when you cannot see clearly the implications of your actions. When you venture forth into the unknown, you learn from the feedback of the physical, emotional and mental levels of your being, how to better align your personal will with your Highest Good. It takes much courage to enter an unknown space, where your choices may bring unexpected consequences. I encourage you to find the positive aspects of each experience, and to give yourself recognition for your courage. Then future activities will prove less fearful for you. This is a very important time on our planet for each of you to make the choice of aligning your personal will with the Divine Will through life experiences. Continue forward courageously on your journey so that you may enhance the lives of others as well as your own.

Spiritual Aspects

Soul Tone: C
Subtle Body Affinities: Emotional/Mental
Element: Fire

Co-creating with Eastern Red Cedar

The cedar family supports you in learning through making choices to align your personal will with your Highest Good. Eastern red cedar encourages you to move into unknown experiences. It dissipates anxiety and fear by letting you know that the important thing is to learn from the consequences. The tangible result is not as important as the quality of the experience and what you learn from it. Eastern red cedar gives courage and tells you to trust your willingness to grow.

Affirmation

"I courageously embrace the unknown and acknowledge every choice as a learning experience."

EASTERN HEMLOCK

Tsuga canadensis

Quality: Openness to Change

Physical Aspects

Look for Eastern hemlock in moist, well-drained sites such as ravines and streambanks, throughout the eastern United States and Canada.

The needles are short and flat, and their undersides are marked by two white lines. They are arranged in two rows on either side of the twig, with a row of upside-down needles flat along the upper side of the twig.

The twig itself is rough, and the tiny, three-quarter-inch cones hang from the tip of the twig. The cones will often remain attached throughout the winter. The bark on young trees is flaky, and becomes more roughly grooved when the tree is older. From a distance the foliage may appear a silvery green, and the bark somewhat iridescent, making this an attractive tree.

Eastern Hemlock

It is important to honor change in your daily life and trust that change broadens your way of knowing. When change occurs, you may discover a complacency that you didn't know you had, and you may feel at times like a victim of life rather than a co-creator of life. This is because the old ways of the past have become more ingrained into your system. I tell you through your energies that the new

patterns that you are hesitant to assimilate are more beneficial for your soul-growth than the old ones. Daily faith is
faith in knowing that all experiences can be integrated
within your being by acknowledging the opportunities that
are present. You may find a new perspective in what at first
seemed impossible, as you look at the situation with the understanding of letting go. Through change you can choose
to deepen your own personal awareness of self and to
strengthen your being. Then you will come to know change
as a freeing of the spirit, and you can chart your course with
a degree of balance within.

Spiritual Aspects

Soul Tone: F
Subtle Body Affinities: Emotional/Mental
Element: Water

Co-creating with Eastern Hemlock

Eastern and Western Hemlock aid you in accepting change in
your life and developing faith. Eastern hemlock contributes to your
emotional balance in the daily circumstances of your life by encouraging you to open to the opportunities for learning. Rather than
questioning or judging events, you accept them with more
equanimity and allow yourself to flow where change takes you.
Eastern hemlock helps dissolve complacency and trying to hold onto
your past ways of doing and understanding things. It aids you in
changing a lack of trust to more acceptance of the flow of events that
are unfolding in your life. Like Western hemlock, it eases the pain
of separation, by returning your focus both to the present moment,
and to the transitory nature of experiences.

Affirmation

"I choose to open to the new opportunities in my changing circumstances."

EASTERN WHITE PINE

Pinus strobus

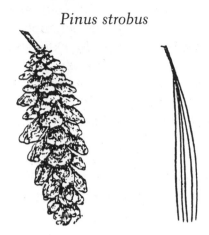

Quality: Becoming Aware of Self-Judgment

Physical Aspects

Eastern white pine is the largest pine of our Eastern forests. You may see it most often in Minnesota, Wisconsin, Michigan and New England. It was much more prolific at one time, but unfortunately it has been extensively lumbered. One way to identify pines is to count the needles, and white pine is the only Eastern pine with needles in bunches of five. These needles are blue-green and three to five inches long.

White pine cones are slender, four to eight inches long, and gracefully curved. If you pick one up, you will most likely find some sticky resin on your hands.

On young pines, the bark is a smooth, greenish brown, but it becomes darker with deep furrows on older trees. White pine branches grow in whorls, about three to seven side branches each year. Thus, you can estimate the age of the tree by counting the whorls, from base to top.

Eastern White Pine Deva

Sometimes you may not realize that you are judging yourself, or setting up expectations of perfection, rather than allowing yourself to be who you are. This is because you have internalized messages from others that are not part of your true self. My energies serve to expand your awareness so that you can see how self-criticism is operating in your life. You can recognize when your thoughts are overly self-critical, by noticing what happens in your body when you think certain thoughts. Does your energy level drop? Do you find yourself feeling irritable or frustrated?

When you deny that a pattern of self-criticism exists, I first bring compassion, and I tell you that a condition is apparent which will require a different perspective than the one you currently hold. I then affirm you as a Divine Being, and I say to you, "Be Yourself As You Truly Are." You then have my support in choosing positive thoughts of self-approval, which promote lightness, cheerfulness and vitality.

Spiritual Aspects

Soul Tone: C
Subtle Body Affinities: Mental
Element: Fire

Co-creating with Eastern White Pine

The pine family helps you to release self-criticism and unrealistic expectations of self. White pine can assist you in becoming aware of how you create unnecessary standards or goals, with resulting anger, depression or low energy. You are then encouraged to build a new definition of yourself that allows you to be less than perfect. As you do this, you will find an increase in overall vitality.

Affirmation

"I acknowledge myself as a lovable and capable person."

LOBLOLLY PINE

Southern Yellow Pine
Pinus taeda

Quality: Emotional Equanimity

Physical Aspects

Loblolly pine is a tall pine of the piedmont and coastal plains of the South, extending as far north as New Jersey. You will also find it in the Mississippi Valley to southwestern Tennessee. It is known for reforesting abandoned fields.

Its needles are five to ten inches long and they grow in bunches of three. The only Southern pine with longer needles is the longleaf pine. The cones are stout, and two-and-one-half to five inches long, with thorn-tipped scales. This cone hurts if you catch one by hand. Its twigs are not as stout as those of the longleaf pine.

Loblolly Pine Deva

When you experience agitation, worry or fear surrounding an experience, it can be difficult to release self-critical attitudes. My energies help to bring you into a space of emotional centeredness and balance that I refer to as equanimity, so that you can heal your relationship with an experience. When you say, ''I just can't seem to think clearly about this situation,'' I tell you to look at how you are feeling at the moment. Through my energies I give you reassurance that aids you in releasing the guilt and self-judgment. I then ask you to examine the experience more deeply by looking at the time preceding it. Quite often the present experience reflects pain from the past that is not healed. My energy supports you in giving to yourself what was needed in the earlier time, as well as what is needed in the present. Once you have moved into a calmer, more positive emotional space, you will then be able to think more clearly and make the choices that you need to make.

Spiritual Aspects

Soul Tone: C
Subtle Body Affinities: Emotional
Element: Fire/Water

Co-creating with Loblolly Pine

When you are agitated, fearful and self-critical about an experience, loblolly pine says something like, "Calm down and relax. Worry will get you nowhere, and things really aren't as bad as they seem." Self-judgment is a kind of emotional rigidity, and loblolly pine offers a flexibility and a touch of humor that helps detach you emotionally from the situation. With more emotional balance, you can choose to let go of judging yourself.

Affirmation

"I regain my emotional balance so that I can let go of self-judgment and choose clearly how to affirm myself."

RED SPRUCE

Picea rubra

Quality: Integrating the Past

Physical Aspects

Red spruce grows in the uplands of the northeastern Appalachians. It is the large spruce that you will see in the Adirondacks of New York, the Green Mountains of Vermont, and the White Mountains of New Hampshire. You might even associate it with cool mountain vacations in the summer.

Its sharp needles are four-sided, stiff, dark green and about one-half-inch long. They often curve forward on the twig. If you pull one off a fallen twig, you will notice that it is attached to a tiny peg which remains, making the twig bumpy to the touch.

The cones are oblong, reddish-brown, and about one to one-and-one-half inches long. These cones remain attached for a few months at the most before they fall. This tree has the rough bark with round scales that is typical of the spruce family.

Red Spruce Deva

In order for you to evolve and grow, it is important to understand the spiritual significance of your experiences. Through my energies you can integrate the positive meaning from your past experiences, so that you have that learning available in your present space. This is easier to do when an experience has been happy or uplifting. When the experience has been difficult, trying to put it out of your mind may isolate you from the pain, but you may also lose the spiritual gift from that experience. When you have not fully integrated the spiritual lessons of your past experiences, it becomes more difficult to accept change, and it is also more difficult to focus on the present. My energies tell you to look for the spiritual wisdom in all experiences, so that you are supported by the spiritual levels of your being.

I encourage you when you are following the practice of seeking spiritual truth through your daily affairs in life, to try to assist others in finding spiritual truth in their lives. When you share the spiritual understanding from a difficult experience, speak from the depth of your heart. In this way you can teach others through your own learning to accept change in life, and to trust that every experience can teach something of value. Each experience contains a seed that can be replanted at a later time to fulfill its growth cycle within you.

Spiritual Aspects

Soul Tone: C
Subtle Body Affinities: Emotional/Mental, Spiritual
Element: Fire/Earth

Co-creating with Red Spruce

The spruce family helps you to connect with your spiritual purpose in life. When you need to understand the significance of a past experience in fulfilling your spiritual purpose you can ask red spruce, "How has that experience broadened my knowledge in my present space?" or "What spiritual qualities was I building at that time?" or "How was this experience fulfilling my life's purpose?" This process will help you to integrate difficult experiences in a more meaningful way into your present understanding, and may help to heal the pain that has kept you focused on the past. Red spruce assists you in seeing your life more as a significant pattern of growth rather than as a collection of unrelated experiences that "just happened."

Affirmation

"I understand how the experiences of the past have contributed to my spiritual growth and purpose in this life."

14 | Oaks, Hickories, Maples, Birches

THIS CHAPTER GROUPS the Eastern oaks, hickories, maples and birches together so that you can see the similarities. You will often find more than one variety of oak and hickory growing together, so that it can be useful to compare their characteristics and qualities.

There are more varieties of oaks in the landscape of our country than any other tree. Simply put, an oak is a tree with an acorn, and almost everywhere you go, you can find a friendly oak. Hickories and maples are often the companions of the oaks. The birches, except for river birch, are northern trees, and are the companions of the Eastern evergreens.

Willow oak and ashleaf maple, or box elder, have not been included in this chapter even though they are botanically members of the oak and maple families. They do not seem to follow the family pattern of qualities, and are unique in themselves, so you will find them in other chapters.

WHITE OAK

Quercus alba

Quality: Steadfast Strength

Physical Aspects

When you think of oak trees, you probably think of the white oak (if you live in the East, that is) because it is the most common and widespread of the oak family. Its bark is the lightest gray of any of the oaks, and the acorn cup is also gray.

White oak leaves have five to nine rounded lobes with smooth tips, while red oak leaves, for example, are bristle-tipped.

If you find a whole acorn, count yourself lucky, because the birds and squirrels are very fond of the nuts. Since it takes fifty years of growth before oaks produce acorns, you will not find them under younger trees. The cup of the acorn is bowl-like and encloses about one fourth of the nut, and the cup scales are warty. When you come to the woods to regain stability and a sense of timelessness, white oak may be right there to welcome you and give you rest.

White Oak Deva

I teach you to work with what is at hand, to create an inner center that is stable and balanced, out of which you grow and serve. Sometimes you may feel discontented because it is difficult for you to accept the rhythms of your life. There is a time for the positive outflow of your energies. However, there is also a time to be still and internalize what has been learned before taking the next step. There is also a time for diversions from your path, to expand how you see yourself. And there is a season of letting go of what was, to make way for what can be. There is wisdom to be learned from each season.

I teach you about the qualities of acceptance and patience, so that you learn not to force change, but to become one with it. You may not have all the answers at any given time, but you can know that you are in a space that is approptiate for you. You develop patience and acceptance through compassion, by affirming your gifts and your talents, and by understanding that you are always learning. My physical form speaks of stable strength, and these qualities I share with you as you align yourself with Divine Will.

Spiritual Aspects

Soul Tone: F
Subtle Body Affinities: Emotional/Mental
Element: Earth/Air

Co-creating with White Oak

The oak family teaches you the power of strength that comes from fully utilizing your inner resources in your current space. White oak gives patience and peace of mind about what is, and perhaps white oak is so common because we need to learn about patience and acceptance. When you feel discontented, pessimistic, or you find yourself impatiently wishing your life were different, white oak calmly centers you, and encourages you to validate your own strength. White oak in particular seems to speak about the rhythms of life, and the balance that involves accepting with compassion the gifts of the present.

Affirmation

"I flow with my current opportunities and accept what is."

RED OAK

Quercus borealis

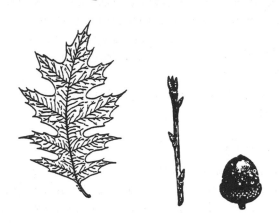

Quality: Resourcefulness

Physical Aspects

Red oak is a large tree that is equally at home in the woods or on city streets. It is one of the more common oaks and thrives in well-drained, sandy soils. It is a member of the "black oak" group along with pin oak. The leaves of this group have bristly tips, which distinguish them from those of the white oak group, whose leaves have rounded tips. The leaves usually have seven to eleven lobes and are thin and smooth, above and below. The mid-rib vein in the middle of the leaf is usually red.

Look for bark that is broken into shiny, flat-topped ridges, as if they had been ironed. The acorn has a shallow, saucer-shaped cup that covers up to one-third of the nut. The cup scales are tight and sometimes fuzzy around the edges. The nut is oblong, and about one inch long. Its white kernel is bitter, unlike white oak acorns.

Red Oak Deva

I encourage you to learn all that you can from a situation so that you develop resourcefulness. When you work with what is at hand, you learn to trust that what is present is sufficient to handle all situations. Sometimes a feeling of lack within self can lead to feeling immobilized or pessimistic about your present situation. My fiery energies encourage you to explore your space, in order to broaden the foundation of your inner center. When you embrace the space in which you find yourself, your increased optimism revitalizes your physical energy. You can seek courage with me, in order to live more fully and robustly.

Spiritual Aspects

Soul Tone: F
Subtle Body Affinities: Emotional/Mental
Element: Earth/Air

Co-creating with Red Oak

The oak family in general tells you that the grass is greener not on the other side of the fence, but right where you are. Red oak energy affirms your skills and talents, and encourages you to be more resourceful. At times you may feel pessimistic, impatient or discouraged because you seem to have exhausted your present possibilities and you really would like to move on. Red oak says cheerfully, "We're not done yet in this space, but look over here at this idea that you didn't see before." Its active energy mobilizes you to affirm yourself more positively, and increases your awareness and enjoyment of what is around you. In this way you learn to explore the endless reservoir of your own ingenuity and strength.

Affirmation

"I flow with my current space and explore my resources more fully."

CHESTNUT OAK

Quercus prinus

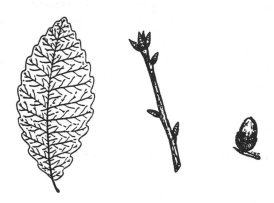

Quality: Focusing on the Present

Physical Aspects

Chestnut oak grows mainly on the poorer, drier soils of hillsides and rocky ridges. The leaves have wavy, regular, smooth edges, like chestnut leaves. They are smooth and somewhat leathery above, and pale and downy beneath.

The bark of the chestnut oak is distinctive with its deep ridges, giving the tree a tough, solid appearance. Chestnut acorns are one-and-one-half to two inches long, making them the largest oak acorns. The cup is thin and encloses about one-third of the nut. The cup scales are tight and knobby, and free at the tips.

Chestnut Oak Deva

Each time that you enter a new experience, you have a choice in how you evaluate what has manifested as well as the resources that you have utilized in the process. If you judge yourself in any manner concerning the resources that you previously utilized or did not utilize, you may find yourself feeling lethargic and entangled in the past. For example, if you must change jobs and are feeling that your skills may no longer be useful, I can help you find ways to integrate those skills into the new situation, so that you see your resources as worthwhile rather than worthless. I can also support you in finding the value in your present moment so that you can shift your focus from regretting the past to finding new possibilities in the present.

I have a closer connection to the life-force energies of your physical vehicle than some other members of the oak family. When you feel an expanding reservoir of energy at your physical level, your powers of concentration are strengthened, and you can connect more strongly with your inner resources.

Spiritual Aspects

Soul Tone: F
Subtle Body Affinities: Emotional/Mental, Etheric
Element: Earth/Air

Co-creating with Chestnut Oak

The oak family helps you develop a core of stable strength that comes from affirming and utilizing your inner resources in whatever situation you happen to be. Chestnut oak can energize physically as well as emotionally, when you are feeling listless, lethargic or despondent as a result of regretting the past. Chestnut oak mobilizes you to accept what may seem to be a loss or change in how you see your resources, so that you become less pessimistic and more optimistic. Its energies can increase your desire to take action with your present resources and to concentrate your strength in the present.

Affirmation

"I integrate into the present the resources that I have developed in the past, so that I can create from a strong inner center."

PIN OAK

Quercus palustris

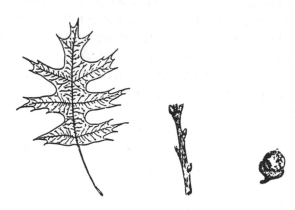

Quality: Hope

Physical Aspects

Pin oak has some of the smallest leaves, buds and acorns of all the native oaks. It gets its name from the slender, pin-like twigs that were used as wooden pegs in the square timbers of old barns. Pin oak is found in poorly drained, flat lowlands, and other wet woodland sites. However, you may first become acquainted with it as a street tree, because it is planted more frequently than any other oak. It is a common oak in the Central states as well as the mid-Atlantic states.

The leaves of pin oak are three to four inches long and bristle-tipped. There are usually very deep spaces between the narrow lobes. In the winter, if you look on the ends of the slender twigs you may see the small, hairless end buds.

The acorn is a useful way of distinguishing the various members of the oak family. The pin oak acorn is about one-half-inch long, with striped, dark lines. The cup is shallow and saucer-shaped, and encloses about one-third of the nut. The cup scales are tight and dark-margined. One other characteristic of the pin oak is that its lower branches droop downward, and dead ones may remain on the tree for many years.

Pin Oak Deva

I help you to understand life's experiences from a higher spiritual perspective, so that you can see the deeper meaning behind your everyday experiences. I teach you through my energies to find the goodness in your present space, and how you are contributing to the greater whole.

Your greatest resource is yourself and your connection to the Infinite Source. As you call forth this Light, you can sense the greater possibilities that are available in the present space, as well as what you are giving to others. Discontent will diminish, and work will seem less burdensome and more comfortable. When you affirm that what you are doing has a far-reaching effect on the quality of all life, you will find peace, reassurance and a renewed appreciation of your own centered strength.

Spiritual Aspects

Soul Tone: F
Subtle Body Affinities: Spiritual, Emotional/Mental
Element: Earth/Air

Co-creating with Pin Oak

Pin oak teaches you to value your inner resources in light of what you are contributing to the Greater Good. If you feel discontented or discouraged and without hope, pin oak lifts you to a more infinite and loving space where you are reassured that everything has a reason even if you can't see it. Pin oak energy is one of the most gentle and peaceful of all the oak energies, connecting you with your own spiritual center so that you can trust your Light and continue on.

Affirmation

"I value my inner resources and the contributions that I am making to the Greater Good."

SHAGBARK HICKORY

Carya ovata

Quality: Organizing with Enthusiasm

Physical Aspects

Shagbark hickory is frequently a companion of white oak, and is found in rich, mature woods and fencerows. Its name comes from the long, gray, loosely attached strips of bark that give this tree a shaggy appearance.

Shagbark leaves are compound and there are usually five leaflets, each four to seven inches long. The terminal leaflet is usually larger than the lateral leaflets. These leaflets have fine-toothed margins and are fragrant when crushed.

In September and October you can find the nut, which is nearly round and one to two-and-one-half inches in diameter. The thick husk splits into four pieces, exposing a sweet, white kernel that squirrels love. Shagbark hickory's end buds are about one-half-inch long with overlapping scales that have sharp projections at their tips. In winter these large end buds are an easy way to identify shagbark hickory.

Shagbark Hickory Deva

Before any action can take place in your physical reality, you must have a clear sense of what you are seeking to accomplish, and also the sequence in which activities are to be done. My energies give you the additional quality of confidence that all the pieces are present for your use and that you can create even more possibilities for manifestation. Confidence is the breeder of enthusiasm, and with enthusiasm comes the pleasure of enjoying the process as well as completing it.

My energies are particularly suited for those times when you may feel a lack of focus or attention for what you are doing. I help you to find the additional meaning in a process so that it becomes more enriching for you.

You must indeed be prepared to commit your understanding into action. I can help you put your knowledge into a usable form that can be shared with others. Knowledge that is integrated through action becomes wisdom that can benefit all forms of life.

Spiritual Aspects

Soul Tone: G
Subtle Body Affinities: Mental
Element: Air/Earth

Co-creating with Shagbark Hickory

The hickory family supports you in prioritizing your thoughts and balancing your mind with a blend of focus and perspective. Shagbark hickory adds an energizing quality of enthusiasm that perks up a lack of interest or a sense of boredom. You may find yourself better able to focus your attention through to completion, and more excited about the planning of your projects.

The enthusiastic quality of shagbark hickory also urges you to put your ideas into action so that you can share your creativity with others. This energy is a blend of confidence, drive and calm perspective that allows you to finish what you start with the overview of purpose always in mind.

Affirmation

"I enthusiastically express my mental wisdom."

PIGNUT HICKORY

Carya glabra

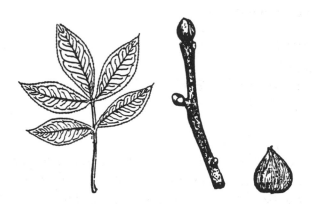

Quality: Timely Manifestation

Physical Aspects

You will find pignut hickory in the drier locations of the Eastern woods. Unlike shellbark hickory, pignut hickory has a smoother bark with tight, irregular, diamond-shaped ridges. Its leaves are compound, usually with five leaflets that are each three to six inches long. The name "pignut" comes from pioneer days when pigs were turned into the woods to eat the nuts. These nuts are thin-shelled, pear-shaped, and about one to two-and-one-half inches long. When ripe, the husk remains closed or partially split. The twigs are hairless and reddish brown, with the smallest end buds of the native hickories.

Pignut Hickory Deva

My energies reassure you of the importance of taking the necessary time to clarify your thinking before you initiate an action. This time is often necessary in order to gather more complete information and to organize the steps needed for a longer range objective. I also encourage you to move beyond hesitation and put your ideas into action when the time is right. If you judge yourself as a "procrastinator," remember that taking time to integrate your information before you take your next step strengthens your confidence and your understanding of the process. This confidence will also help you act with decisiveness when you have the information that you need. The result is that you move forward in a timely fashion with every experience that you have in life.

Spiritual Aspects

Soul Tone: G
Subtle Body Affinities: Mental
Element: Air/Earth

Co-creating with Pignut Hickory

The hickory family helps you clarify and prioritize your thinking. In addition, pignut hickory heightens your sense of timing, so that you understand better when to wait and plan, and when to act. Its active energy encourages you to make a decision and manifest a goal, when you have been hesitating or drifting.

Affirmation

"I listen to my inner direction on when it is time to wait and plan, and when it is time to act."

RED MAPLE

Swamp Maple, Soft Maple
Acer rubrum

Quality: Enjoying Your Unique Self

Physical Aspects

Red maple thrives on both swampy and dry sites. Its name is justified because it gives us red all year around. In the spring the flowers burst forth in short clusters of gauzy red, tiny blossoms. The summer fruits are red, and in the fall the leaves turn brilliant crimsons and yellows. After the leaves are down, look for reddish twigs and buds. The twigs do not have an odor when broken, as do the silver maple twigs.

Red maple leaves are usually three-lobed, although sometimes they have five lobes. They differ from sugar maple leaves in that the lobes are shallowly cut, and the angle between the lobes is in the shape of a V. When you look up, you might see the whitened undersides of these leaves, and of course, their red stems.

Red Maple Deva

You have much that you can give to other lifestreams, as well as receive from them. When you feel shy or reticent, or you have chosen to avoid contact with others, my energies encourage your desire for movement out of yourself and into the world of others. The purpose of sharing with someone else is to broaden your own unique sense of who you are, through the eyes of another, and to do likewise for that person. Through my energies you affirm your own uniqueness and joyfully share yourself with others. When you find the virtues that are present within your own being, you have the keys to more beautiful relationships with others.

Spiritual Aspects

Soul Tone: D
Subtle Body Affinities: Emotional/Mental
Element: Fire

Co-creating with Red Maple

Red maple cheers you on to affirm yourself and share your gifts with others. You may especially need to do this when you feel like avoiding others after experiencing a hurt or a disappointment. Red maple says, "This is a new beginning. Put your best foot forward and everything will be fine." Red maple also encourages an outgoing interest in others, and an enjoyment in relationships. If you are shy, or uncertain about your social skills, red maple is a delightful confidence-booster.

Affirmation

"I share my special Light with others, and enjoy my expansion."

SUGAR MAPLE

Hard Maple, Rock Maple
Acer saccarum

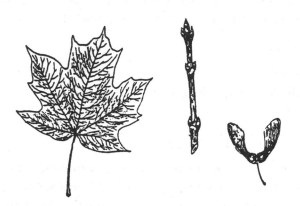

Quality: Affirming Others

Physical Aspects

Although sugar maple is found throughout the northeastern two-thirds of the United States, we often think of it as a New England tree. In the fall, the sugar maple leaves turn the most brilliant reds of any broadleaf tree.

The bark is a dark gray with ridges and thick, curled plates. Sugar maple leaves have five lobes, and the angle between each lobe forms a U. The edges are smooth and the leaf itself is bright green above, and a smooth, paler green underneath.

The maple family is also known for its two-winged seeds, which look like opening scissor blades as they mature in the autumn. In the winter, sugar maple twigs shine with their reddish-brown, glossy bark, and their sharp, pointed bud scales. Many think that the sugar maple is one of the most beautiful trees in the world.

Sugar Maple Deva

Each time you have an interaction with another person, look for the qualities that radiate Light from that being, and that warm your heart inside. You see, the more that you call forth the Light within others, the more their Light enriches you. Let your continuing affirmation be that you will honor each beautiful facet of another being, and reflect those facets back to that being. You will find that your life becomes filled with pleasure and joy, as you open to the surprises in others and to the spontaneity in yourself. My sweet sap symbolizes the flow of Unconditional Love that blesses your life as you share that flow with others.

Spiritual Aspects

Soul Tone: D
Subtle Body Affinities: Emotional/Mental
Element: Fire

Co-creating with Sugar Maple

Sugar maple teaches you how to affirm others by mirroring to them their unique, beautiful qualities. When you feel disappointed or frustrated with others, or stuck in seeing only the unhealed places, sugar maple moves your focus to their positive qualities.

Its energies also release despondency by encouraging you to play with others, and to find pleasure in sharing joy together. Sugar maple heightens the connection between pleasure, and the giving and receiving of Unconditional Love.

Affirmation

"I honor you and I rejoice in your special gifts."

SILVER MAPLE

White Maple
Acer saccharinum

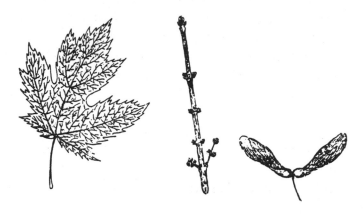

Quality: Healing Disappointment in Relationships

Physical Aspects

Silver maple grows in the moist, rich soils of the eastern United States, and has been popular as a shade tree. The leaves of the silver maple are more deeply lobed than the sugar maple leaves, and are white and downy underneath. Silver maple bark is dark gray, and broken into long, flaky strips on old trees.

The two-winged seeds are the largest of the maple seeds, with the wings spread wide apart. The seeds grow in clusters, and so do the flower buds which you can spot in the winter.

Silver Maple Deva

My energies span the entire arena of relationships, from those of a temporary nature, to those of a longer duration. Each time you enter into a relationship, you bring with you expectations concerning the focus and quality of your interactions. When that relationship terminates, you may find yourself feeling disappointed, frustrated or disillusioned if your expectations were not met. You cannot choose the actions of another being, but you can choose how you respond to your loss and disappointment.

I help you to focus on the positive qualities of the other person. When you reflect Light into another, that Light is received by the other, as well as by you, the sender. When you know that you have given Unconditional Love to another, you also become aware of ways in which you have become stronger in your own sense of self through the relationship. The flow of Unconditional Love strengthens your capacity to heal in your relationships and to move into new ones. In relationships you learn how to assimilate the highest form of vibration from another into your own being, so that you are strengthened and expanded.

Spiritual Aspects

Soul Tone: D
Subtle Body Affinities: Emotional/Mental
Element: Fire

Co-creating with Silver Maple

Silver maple helps you release disappointment and disillusionment at a change in form or the termination of a relationship. You are encouraged to extend Unconditional Love to the other by affirming the positive qualities of that person. Silver maple also tells you to focus Unconditional Love toward yourself and affirm your own gifts to the relationship. As you do this you will experience more peace. When you are feeling lonely, as though you have been cast adrift into the sea, silver maple reminds you that your Unconditional Love for another always connects you with that person, and comforts you with your own strength.

Affirmation

"Your Light is always with me, showing me my path toward Unconditional Love and Inner Peace."

RIVER BIRCH

Red Birch
Betula nigra

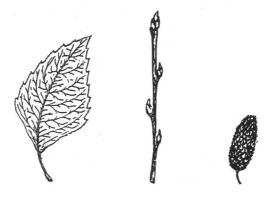

Quality: Risking in Relationships

Physical Aspects

River birch grows along streambanks, ponds or rivers in the eastern third of our country. It is the South's only real birch, and it is the birch that prefers wet ground. The members of the birch family are often noted for their distinctive bark. River birch has shaggy, cinnamon-red bark, which peels off in strips on younger trees. The bark on old trees becomes dark-colored and rough. River birch often divides near its base into two slender trunks.

The leaves are one-and-one-half to three inches long, double-toothed, and wedge-shaped at the base. Sometimes the undersides will be whitish and velvety underneath. The broken twigs do not taste of wintergreen as do the twigs of sweet and yellow birches.

River Birch Deva

When you have been somewhat of a loner, or if you have been hurt in a previous relationship, you may fear being vulnerable again. When there is a call within your being to extend yourself to another, I can help you initiate that process with more trust.

If you fear being rejected or ignored, I tell you through my energies to share a small part of yourself that you feel most comfortable in sharing with another. It is O.K. to take one step at a time and build compatibility slowly. Remember that no two beings are exactly alike, and if you look, you will find qualities that will lay the ground work for developing a successful relationship. I also help you not to lose sight of the positive things that you have learned in your previous relationships so that you can build the new relationship with your affirmations.

In order to trust again, you must release your past experience so that you do not judge the current relationship with past perspectives. There is risk involved in initiating a relationship, but I say that you can move forward with that risk, and make something special out of what seems to be a challenge in the beginning. I can give you the support you need to trust your new space, and I welcome you to new enrichment in your life.

Spiritual Aspects

Soul Tone: F
Subtle Body Affinities: Emotional/Mental
Element: Water/Air

Co-creating with River Birch

The birch family focuses on healing relationships, both intimate family relationships and less personal friendships. River birch could be called "the honeymoon tree." When you are considering whether or not to enter more deeply into a relationship, it shares qualities of vision and delight that can mobilize you to take the plunge. River birch can help dissolve fears of being ignored, rejected or vulnerable to hurt. It reminds you of the joy in sharing with another and tells you that the difficulties can be transcended. It also says that much pleasure awaits you as you trust and open yourself to the process.

Affirmation

"I now risk opening myself to a new relationship, and trust that I am being supported in this experience."

YELLOW BIRCH

Silver Birch
Betula lutea

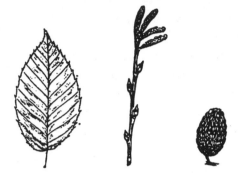

Quality: Acceptance of Others in Relationships

Physical Aspects

You will see yellow birch in the Great Lakes region, New England, and the Appalachians, often with beech, sugar maple, hemlock and black birch. It grows to a larger size than other members of the birch family. Its bark is a glossy, silvery bronze that peels into small, thin curls.

The leaves are similar to those of black birch, with a base that may be heart-shaped or rounded. Another similarity with black birch is that both trees have twigs that taste of wintergreen.

The oval fruit catkins that grow from August to October remain erect, and shed their seed slowly. The sketch shows the winter twig with buds and partially grown female flowers. If you need to build a campfire in the rain, look for fallen yellow birch bark, because it will burn even when it is wet, due to the oils in its bark.

Yellow Birch Deva

In your world you often create beliefs about another person based on your first impressions. If this person has a different ethnic background, economic status, or a physical disability, you may close your mind to the positive nature within this person. Or perhaps another being presents a cold, aloof front, or has strange ways of behaving and you find yourself judging this person's behavior.

My energies tell you to go beyond the first impressions and to step closer to that person. Look for the qualities and gifts that this person has to extend to you, and to others. When you broaden your viewpoint of the reality of others' lives without judgment, you can open to another person more fully, and you will find yourself more relaxed in interpersonal relationships. You will come to know more interesting people with a wide range of awareness and understanding. When you give another being the chance to be seen for who he or she really is, you open the way for that person to perceive your special qualities. To give and receive compassion is truly your purpose for being on the Earth plane.

Spiritual Aspects

Soul Tone: F
Subtle Body Affinities: Mental/Emotional
Element: Water/Air

Co-creating with Yellow Birch

Yellow birch helps you to move beyond stereotyping another person, to finding the special gifts with which he or she serves you. In more intimate relationships, yellow birch asks you to look beyond the personal idiosyncrasies or annoying mannerisms that may keep you focused on trying to change that person. If you bask in the Light of your friend, that which you find difficult to accept dims considerably. Yellow birch asks you to accept others, and move always toward Oneness, and away from separateness.

Affirmation

"In relationships, I accept others for who they are without judgment, as I wish to be accepted."

BLACK BIRCH

Sweet Birch, Cherry Birch
Betula lenta

Quality: Confronting Self in Relationships

Physical Aspects

Black birch grows in the Appalachian forests and the Great Lakes region. On young trees the bark is dark brown, smooth, glossy, and peppered with white dashes, like cherry bark. As the tree ages the bark breaks into large plates. Black birch twigs have a distinctive wintergreen taste, and the oil of wintergreen is distilled commercially from the bark and twigs.

Black birch leaves are oval-shaped and more elongated than paper birch leaves, with unevenly toothed edges. If you look underneath, the color will be yellowish-green, with some white hairs growing at the points where the veins join. The base is heart-shaped, whereas the paper birch leaf has a rounded base. After being pollinated by the long male catkins, the small female fruiting catkins create cone-like structures that are about one-and-one-half inches long. These cony seed tassels remain on the tree all winter, scattering the tiny, winged nuts on the snow for the birds to eat.

Black Birch Deva

Intimate relationships are an opportunity to deepen your self-awareness and to contribute to the personal growth of another as well as your own growth. A conflict or a disagreement can be a catalyst for that growth, because its resolution often requires that you examine how your beliefs and attitudes are impacting on the other person. In resolving a conflict or an imbalance, I first tell you that pointing a finger of blame at another for the lack of communication is not the answer. Instead, try to find wherein your attitudes you may be rigid or judgmental. Stop thinking that you need to change another person's way of seeing things. This is an opportunity to work on your own perception of things.

It is also necessary to look at the experience not only from your perspective, but through the eyes of the other. Quite often, what is required is a closer listening to what is actually being said, rather than a drawing of conclusions as to what you think is meant. This is how you honor another person's space as well as your own.

Explore the common ground of similarities in your thoughts and feelings, so that you can create a stronger foundation on which to build. Each of you has pieces to the puzzle known as life. By allowing others to fit their pieces into the puzzle along with your own, the picture that emerges is more clear and complete. Fulfillment comes as you integrate the gift of truth into your being, and allow yourself to nurture and be nurtured by those gifts.

Spiritual Aspects

Soul Tone: F
Subtle Body Affinities: Emotional/Mental
Element: Water/Air

Co-creating with Black Birch

The birch family assists you in better understanding your relationships. Black birch can give you feedback on how you are contributing to imbalance in an intimate relationship. For example, when I lean up against it, I have learned that in times of conflict I tend to overprotect others in order to keep the peace. Black birch takes you inward and asks you to look at where you need to grow.

Affirmation

"I open to what I need to learn in order to build a stronger intimate relationship."

PAPER BIRCH

White Birch, Canoe Birch
Betula papyrifera

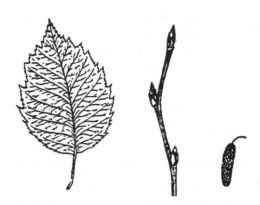

Quality: Reconciliation in Relationships

Physical Aspects

You may associate paper birch with snow because this is a northern tree, found from New England south to Pennsylvania, and across Michigan, Minnesota and into Alaska. Its beauty is perhaps its chalky, white bark, which can be peeled off in sheets. Once the white bark is peeled off, the orange inner bark is exposed, and the tree will never grow white bark over that spot again. Many paper birches have been damaged by people who have thoughtlessly peeled the bark off the tree. This bark is smooth, waterproof and tough, which is why it was ideal for Native American canoes.

The leaves, which are uniformly oval and sharply double-toothed, grow from reddish-brown twigs. In autumn, paper birch bears immature catkins which can remain on the tree throughout the winter in order to produce seeds in the spring.

Paper Birch Deva

In Nature, the philosophy of life is that *you are who you are and I am who I am, and neither of us has to justify our own being.* Each species has a sensitivity and an awareness of the space where it is, and does the best that it can in its own unique growth. At no time does any species adopt a competitive or aggressive attitude that says, "I am *better* than you." When you of the Human Kingdom substitute cooperation for competition, you will find that your relationships flow in a more natural rhythm, based on the acceptance of others.

However, you have not yet completely learned this lesson, and since you have the gift of free will, you have at times chosen to experience direct confrontation with another human being. I can teach you about the process of reconciliation. An unresolved conflict means that the energies are stuck, so that what is needed is a movement of energies between the people involved. The truth is like a diamond with many facets. Each of you is looking at a different facet of the diamond. Be willing to accept that what the other person says has validity, if not for yourself, then for that person. This will be easier to do if you seek the God Within the other person, beyond the personality or ego. Listen with your heart to what the other person is saying, rather than with your ego in your determination to be right. The heart-centered space is one of trying to understand why another believes as he or she does. When you listen from your heart and say honestly, ''I am willing to think about that,'' then you have moved beyond the placating that is part of a strategy of attack and defense.

As you look for the God-self within the other person, you must also honor your own God-self. Reconciliation means honoring your own way of being, and finding the solution that allows each or you your uniqueness. I tell you through my energies that there does not need to be a loser in a disagreement. If you focus on losing and winning, you can sabotage the work that has been done in building trust. Instead there can be a positive sense of possibility that each of you takes within him or herself, whether or not there has been an overt shift in perspective.

The key to reconciliation is in the movement of energy, which can take the form of increased awareness for each of you. When you open yourself to hear, and when you listen from your heart, you will be richer from what you have shared. Change often does not take place instantaneously, and so it is necessary to release your own expectations of what you hope will happen. Give the process the time and space that you deserve.

Your Planet is an extension of how you relate to other people in your everyday world. The more that you are able to work in a difficult space with others in seeking the reconciliation of your disagreements, the more peace you will find on your Planet, and the more healing will take place in all kingdoms.

Spiritual Aspects

Soul Tone: F
Subtle Body Affinities: Emotional/Mental
Element: Water/Air

Co-creating with Paper Birch

If you are having a disagreement with someone, join him or her in leaning up against a paper birch. Ask for Unconditional Love from the tree, and then connect in Unconditional Love with your partner. Paper birch supports you in creating a greater balance between your solar plexus and your heart, so that you can strengthen your belief in who you are and at the same time accept others for who they are. You are encouraged to communicate from the heart and to recognize what is significant, and what is not important. Paper birch can also assist you in seeing more clearly where there is agreement and understanding. It speaks of valuing harmony above pride.

When you visualize world peace, you can infuse the energies of paper birch into the hearts of the leaders, or image the leaders negotiating inside a circle of paper birch trees. Affirm that peace is now unfolding from a space of Unity and Oneness within each heart, and in the hearts of all humankind.

Affirmation

"I seek greater awareness, trust and harmony in all my relationships."

GRAY BIRCH

White Birch
Betula populifolia

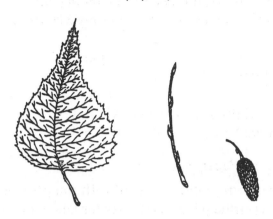

Quality: Separation in Relationships

Physical Aspects

You may have already spotted gray birch, if you live around New York City, Washington, D.C., Baltimore or Philadelphia. It is a tree of the northeastern woods, which some people refer to as white birch because the bark is white. However, it is a dull or silvery white, rather than the snowy white of paper birch. Also, the bark does not readily peel into paper-thin sheets. It is usually marked by many conspicuous black triangles, where the branches have broken off.

The leaves are different from paper birch leaves. They are triangular, with a long, tapering point, rather than oval like paper birch leaves. The fruiting catkins are short, about three-quarters of an inch long.

Gray Birch Deva

Sometimes relationships continue beyond their needed time because neither you nor the other being has been willing to take responsibility for its termination. Through my energies I encourage you to do so, when the learning process in this relationship is complete. For in truth, the longer a relationship goes beyond its purpose, the more difficult it becomes to complete it. Perhaps the hardest part is healing the sense of loss at the end of a relationship, and I can help to comfort your grief. I encourage you to take time to focus your attention on the positive experiences that you have shared with this person. How has this being enriched your life? How are you different from having been in the space with this being? Allow time for the healing and the assimilation of the goodness that has taken place from the relationship, before you try to fill the empty space inside of you with a new relationship. If you merely seek to replace the old relationship with a new one, you will create expectations that limit your new relationship. It is important to take what you have learned and put it into practical application in your life. In this way, you can heal the sadness of ending, and truly honor the relationship through personal action. Support is always with you to guide each of you along the unique path of your soul's journey.

Spiritual Aspects

Soul Tone: F
Subtle Body Affinities: Emotional/Mental
Element: Water/Air

Co-creating with Gray Birch

The birch family aids you in developing better relationships, and gray birch assists you in looking at what you are learning in your relationship. Sometimes what you need is to release certain expectations that you may have had about the relationship. If your sense is that the learning is complete, gray birch supports you in detaching from the relationship so that you can better understand and accept a decision to separate. It also gives comfort and support when you fear that loss and emptiness may overwhelm you if you decide to separate. Gray birch teaches that the ending of relationships is part of the cycle of growth in relationships, and that ending can be accomplished by focusing on the positive nature of that growth.

Affirmation

"I am healed by focusing on the positive nature of what I am learning in all stages of my relationships."

15 | More Eastern Trees

Perhaps you have a memory of picnicking in a town park under friendly, old trees, which spoke of coolness and comfort. They might have been beeches, elms, ashes or black walnuts, which can all grow quite large.

The trees in this chapter such as sycamore and tulip poplar are often easy to identify because they are one of a kind. The following poem could have been written about any one of these trees:

> We stand in awe and wonder
> at the beauty of a single tree.
> Tall and graceful it stands, yet robust and sinewy
> with spreading arms decked with foliage
> that changes through the seasons, hour by hour,
> moment by moment as the shadows pass
> or sunshine dapples the leaves.
> —Richard St. Barbe Baker

WHITE ASH

American Ash
Fraxinus americana

Quality: Clarification of Values

Physical Aspects

You will find the white ash, the largest native variety of ash, growing in the rich soils of the Eastern woods. Ash leaves are compound, like walnut and hickory. The leaflets grow opposite each other on short stalks and are each three to five inches long. The name "white ash" comes from the white undersides of the leaflets. The bark of the white ash is generally dark with uniform ridges that form a tight, diamond pattern.

In winter, you can identify a white ash by the distinguishing characteristics of the twigs. These twigs are round, heavy and hairless, with leaf buds that grow opposite each other.

The winged seeds produced by the female tree are sometimes called "keys," and look like canoe paddles. They hang in large clusters and may remain attached to the tree for several months in autumn.

White Ash Deva

What you clarify through my energies is what particular values and thought patterns are in harmony with your spiritual nature. I create a space of detachment from your emotional energies so that you can know what is true for you. Sometimes your mind becomes clouded and confused with beliefs that you have learned from others and which are not in alignment with your Divinity. I help you assess your thinking from a space of calm serenity and a purity of awareness. When you allow your spiritual nature to assist you, you move from a space of constricted thinking to a more expanded thinking that creates a sense of integrated well-being.

Spiritual Aspects

Soul Tone: G
Subtle Body Affinities: Mental, Spiritual
Element: Air

Co-creating with White Ash

White ash detaches you from your emotions and connects you with your spiritual nature in a mental space that is still and serene. When you feel confused about what you want for yourself, white ash energy can help you clarify what is true for you. When what you believe is in harmony with your spiritual nature, you may feel a calm, expanded sense of certainty in your decision-making that can be very reassuring.

Affirmation

"I open my mind to my spiritual nature in order to clarify my beliefs and make clear decisions."

BEECH

Fagus grandifolia

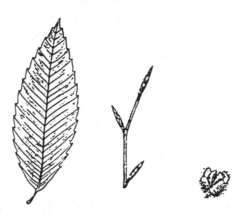

Quality: Tolerance

Physical Aspects

When you see beech trees, you know that you are in a mature forest. Beech can be recognized at any time of the year by its silvery-gray, smooth bark.

The leaves are a bright, glossy green with prominent, parallel veins. Each leaf is three to five inches long, with conspicuous, sharp teeth. In the fall, the leaves turn a golden brown and remain on the tree all winter, especially on young trees.

The beech buds are one inch long, which is unusually long for a bud, and very pointed. The prickly burr husks usually enclose two triangular nuts which are sweet, and therefore prized by squirrels, deer and birds.

Beech Deva

Tolerance begins with self, when you view yourself in Oneness with others, rather than separated from them. The sense of unity comes from the knowledge that all forms of life have One Source of Energy. You are intolerant when you restrict your path to one predominant point of view that does not honor the Spiritual Source that overlights all. I assist you into a more harmonious state with your Spiritual Self so that you are then more tolerant of the paths which others choose to follow in order to reach their own sense of Divine Self. There are truly many pathways to Divine Oneness with Self. When you can accept the paths that others have chosen, you are also in a space to learn from their experiences as well as your own. You will also receive a greater inflow of life-force energies, bringing understanding and greater balance to your being.

Spiritual Aspects

Soul Tone: A
Subtle Body Affinities: Emotional/Mental
Element: Air

Co-creating with Beech

If you are fearful or angry about the path that another person has chosen, beech connects you more deeply into a space of greater compassion so that you can accept another's decisions with tolerance and understanding.

Beech can assist you in releasing beliefs about spirituality that you adopted when you were younger, but which may not serve you appropriately now. Its energy is gentle and very expansive, asking you to seek wisdom in all people and all experiences, and to be guided by the underlying Oneness of All Life.

Affirmation

"I affirm that many paths lead to Wisdom, and I treat others with tolerance and understanding."

FLOWERING DOGWOOD

Cornus florida

Quality: Seeing Beauty in All Things

Physical Aspects

You may not notice the small flowering dogwoods scattered throughout the Eastern United States, except in the spring before the leaves come out. Particularly from the mid-Atlantic region southward, the dogwoods light up the woods with white blossoms. Technically these are not considered flowers, but bracts. The tiny "true" flowers are clustered in the center, surrounded underneath by four large, white bracts, which used to be the bud scales.

Dogwood is also showy in the fall, with lovely red clusters of two to five berries that remain on the tree for a while after the leaves fall. The bark has a checkered appearance that reminds some people of alligator skin.

Flowering Dogwood Deva

I ask you to open your eyes and your heart to the beauty in Nature. Open all the senses of your being, as I call upon you to touch my leaves and enjoy my bright colors. As you explore the physical form of my flowers, leaves and berries, you are stimulated to appreciate the beauty created by Nature and by the Human Kingdom as well.

Notice how a particular species integrates with other species to form a balanced pattern of symmetry. How are you as a divine creation of beauty blending into your personal space? This is not a question of judgment but rather a question of self-assessment. Feel your own personal beauty, and how it contributes to the quality of life around you. Beauty is an act of creation, and you are both the creator and the creation in all that you do.

When you love someone you are appreciating and honoring the beauty that is expressed by that person. Beauty is appreciated through the heart, and when you open your heart, you allow yourself to receive a precious and sacred gift. Let this gift be a catalyst for you to further commit to the deepening of your own inner beauty.

Spiritual Aspects

Soul Tone: D#
Subtle Body Affinities: Emotional/Mental
Element: Water

Co-creating with Flowering Dogwood

Flowering dogwood heightens your aesthetic appreciation of your environment. Sometimes losing your connection with Nature by being indoors for long periods of time, for example, can bring a numbness or an insensitivity to your surroundings. Dogwood energy activates you to take an increased interest in what you see around you and to enjoy yourself.

When you have withdrawn from others after a deep hurt, dogwood gently opens your senses so that Nature can heal you. A deepening aesthetic appreciation can also lead you to reach out to others with more sensitivity, and to appreciate beauty in others wherever you find it.

Affirmation

"I honor the beauty that is all around me, as well as my own beauty."

AMERICAN ELM

Ulmus americana

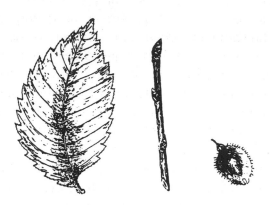

Quality: Compassionate Self-Honesty

Physical Aspects

The American elm is considered by many to be a lovely, graceful tree that thrives in scattered locations on a variety of soils. Stately, old elms provide shade in fields, meadows, woods and city streets throughout the Middle West as well as the East.

The trunk usually splits near the ground into several large branches that fan outward in a vase-like shape which attracts the eye.

The leaf is also unique in that it is usually distinctly lopsided or asymmetrical at its base, with a pointed tip and double-toothed margins. You may find this leaf sandpapery to the touch, although the leaves vary in their smoothness.

American elm bark is dark gray, with broken, diamond-shaped, lacy ridges. In April or May you may find the one-half-inch-long seeds surrounded by thin, papery wings. Both flowers and seeds appear before the leaves.

A certain leaf-hopping insect carries a virus known as the Dutch Elm disease, which destroys the bark of the elm. Our elms, unfortunately, continue to succumb to this disease.

American Elm Deva

I work through your heart center, for that is where you learn trust and compassion for self and others. It is important to seek a balance between giving to others and caring for your own personal needs. Caring for self is one facet of compassion, as caring for others is another facet.

I teach you about the quality of honesty with self. When you have defined generosity as giving to others, while at the same time devaluing your own needs, I ask you to be true to your heart. When giving becomes a burden of responsibility, you may find that you are trying to become more than you are. This outward focus, which does not include acknowledging your inner needs, may lead to disillusionment and disconnection with your true nature.

Honesty and self-understanding are best achieved when your thoughts and feelings are turned within, where the Light is always present. When you grow into the awareness of our own value, you also deepen your understanding of compassion, which rests in accepting your Inner Divinity.

Spiritual Aspects

Soul Tone: F#
Subtle Body Affinities: Emotional/Mental
Element: Earth

Co-creating with American Elm

American elm teaches you about compassion for self as well as others, by asking you to look at your motivation for giving to others. Do you want to be liked? Are other people more important than you are? Do you have a belief that it is "selfish" to give to yourself and "self-less" to give to others?

Amerian elm supports you in valuing yourself and your needs. Its energies draw you inward to strengthen your caring for yourself and to *be* rather than *do*. When you learn greater self-awareness and honesty, your compassion for self deepens, and you give to others from the greater nurturing of the Light Within.

Affirmation

"I am honest with myself about who I am, what my needs are, and what I can do."

BLACK LOCUST

Robinia pseudoacacia

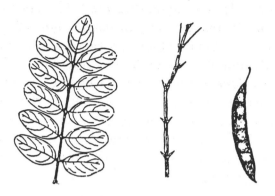

Quality: Assessment Without Judgment

Physical Aspects

Black locust is a tree of the fields as well as the woods, and you will find it in every Eastern state but Florida. It was originally native to the southern Appalachians, but settlers planted it widely because the wood makes tough fenceposts.

When this tree finally decides to bloom in the spring, look for compound leaves with seven to nineteen egg-shaped leaflets. The bark of an old locust is deeply furrowed and rugged in appearance, with disorganized ridges. The twigs are lined with short, stout thorns. You may be drawn to the black locust in the summer by its fragrant flowers that look like sweet peas. These flowers produce three-inch-long, dark, flat pods that ripen in September and October. They will flutter on the tree all winter.

Black Locust Deva

You can live your life without blaming others for your experiences, or feeling victimized by outside circumstances. You have a choice in how you think about an experience. You can reflect on what has been positive for you, or you can concentrate on what has been absent or lacking in the experience. This is blame, when you focus on the limitations of others because your own expectations have not been met. When you are judgmental, you create a resistance to change which keeps you stuck in one way of perceiving things, and you do not grow.

Releasing blame is first of all honestly examining your own actions. Then it is necessary to take responsibility for your actions by being willing to assess alternative ways of being. You may blame others because it is difficult for you to accept your own limitations. You can release self-judgment by looking for the positive features in yourself and the experience. Once you have a better understanding of why things are the way they are, my energies can help you disengage from the past. You will then have more clarity in knowing the alternative actions you can take in the present and future.

Spiritual Aspects

Soul Tone: D#
Subtle Body Affinities: Emotional/Mental
Element: Fire

Co-creating with Black Locust

When you feel like blaming your environment or other people for a situation in which you currently find yourself, black locust helps you to see the situation from a point of view where you can take responsibility for your actions. This often means claiming your own power inside yourself, and being willing to make changes. Its quality is cathartic when you have avoided dealing with an issue, and supportive when you wish to take alternative steps. Black locust encourages you to grow, even when it is difficult.

Affirmation

"I assess my actions without judgment, and I take responsibility for them, without blaming others."

SWEETGUM

Redgum
Liquidamber styraciflua

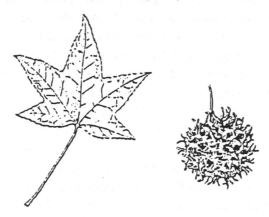

Quality: Initiative, Involvement, Completion

Physical Aspects

Sweetgum grows from southern Connecticut to Florida and west as far as Texas and southeastern Missouri. It is most common in the South where, in the fall, its wine-red foliage brightens the more subdued yellows and greens.

Sweetgum leaves are star-shaped, usually with five and sometimes seven lobes. The lobes are arranged like a six-pointed star, with the stem where the sixth lobe would be. The bark is a soft gray with regular furrows. Sweetgum gets its name from the fragrant resin that oozes from wounds. This thick resin can be chewed, like chewing gum. In the fall, when you are not looking up at the leaves, you can look down on the ground and collect the woody seed balls. These little balls are covered with curved points and make imaginative Christmas decorations. In the winter sweetgum is easily identified by its corky, winged twigs.

Sweetgum Deva

Everything that you do in your life has energy patterns of its own. I encourage you to heighten the quality of involvement in your activities. Sometimes the hardest thing is for you to get started. You may tell yourself that it really does not matter whether or not you do something, because the activity has no real meaning in your life. Or you may be in a space of inertia where you are detached from what is happening in your life. When you have difficulty initiating an activity, you are like a car battery that is unconnected. I first connect you to your power source, which is the meaning an activity can have in your life. Then I turn on the starter of interest and involvement, so that you can enjoy it to your fullest capacity. For example, if you decide to plant a rosebush in your yard, you can appreciate the role of the nutrients that you are adding to the soil in preparation for the plant's growth. You can also appreciate the beauty of the rosebush in its present state while you are planting it. As you notice how the rosebush adds to the balance of your environment, and visualize how it will look in full bloom, you will have increased your enjoyment of the process of planting. By finding pleasure in each step of the process, and completely involving your emotional, mental, and spiritual resources, you will experience a deepened fulfillment in the completion of your activity. I encourage you to act rather than wait, and to participate with attention and enthusiasm in whatever you do.

Spiritual Aspects

Soul Tone: D
Subtle Body Affinities: Emotional/Mental
Element: Fire

Co-creating with Sweetgum

Sweetgum balances inertia and hesitancy with the desire to get started and get things done. If you are experiencing ambivalence or a lack of interest in your activities, sweetgum heightens your involvement so that you can find more meaning in what you are doing. Sweetgum also strengthens your momentum in completing a project by increasing your sense of fulfillment in what is being accomplished. Sweetgum aids procrastinators by saying, "Do it now, you will be glad you did." It encourages you to be creative, rather than mechanical with your daily activities.

Affirmation

"My time is now, and I start and finish my activities with deeper enthusiasm and involvement."

SYCAMORE

American Plane Tree, Buttonball-tree
Platanus occidentalis

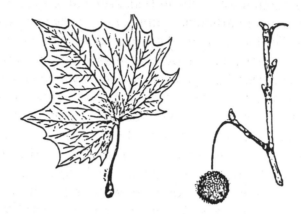

Quality: Concern for the Quality of All Life

Physical Aspects

While tulip tree is generally considered to be the tallest Eastern forest tree, the sycamore is probably the most massive Eastern tree. The largest sycamores live in the Mississippi and Ohio river basins, and you will probably find them along any lowland riverbank.

The sycamore is known for its bark, which is mottled like that of Pacific madrone. It grows an inner layer of bark each year, and the outer layer, which does not grow, peels off in brown flakes. The inner bark becomes white as it is exposed to the sun, so sycamore bark is patchy brown, yellow and white, with white upper branches.

The leaves are four to seven inches across, with three to five lobes. There are two to three coarse teeth to the inch, and the leaf usually feels woolly underneath. If you carefully pluck a leaf from its twig, you will notice that the leaf stalk base is hollow, and covers a bud in the winter.

The sycamore is an American relative of the European London plane tree, which is also planted as a street tree in this country. Sycamores grow a one-inch "fruit," commonly known as a buttonball, which hangs singly on a tough, slender stalk. The London plane tree will usually have two or more balls in clusters, and its bark patches are brown rather than white.

Sycamore Deva

When you look to others or society as a yardstick to measure how you need to be in the world, you truly restrict the fullest expression of the individuality that is your service. When you wear particular clothing principally because it is the latest fashion, you are denying who you are. When you eat certain foods because others are eating them, you deny your own physical being its unique needs. When your world communicates to you that it is not the right time for you to do a certain thing, and you choose to go along with what is being said, you deny your ability to think independently and honor your own timing. Your actions need to be independent of what other people decide to do with their lives. Remember that no one can walk your path for you, and no one walks their path in the same manner that you are walking yours. When you keep this thought in mind, it is easier to choose during those times when you anticipate feeling a bit separated from the world as a result of your choices.

When you are living your uniqueness, I tell you that other humans as well as Nature benefit from your actions. To ''do what everyone else does'' can mean living in a space of inertia. If, for example, you decide to pick up rubbish from the side of the road, I can show you what it would be like if all people cleaned up their garbage, so that you are motivated to take further individual action. Let the trust that you know from your heart, rather than the need for approval from others, guide your actions. Every small change becomes itself part of a new pattern that impacts on more life forms. Then, when you carry out your actions with thoughts of giving love and service to others, your activities will have meaning and enjoyment for you, and you will make a difference in the quality of life for all species on this planet.

Spiritual Aspects

Soul Tone: D#
Subtle Body Affinities: Emotional/Mental
Element: Water/Fire

Co-creating with Sycamore

Sycamore gives childlike qualities of gentleness and joy that encourage you to create a more caring environment for others in everything that you do. When you feel a sense of stagnation, a lack of interest in your daily life, as though you were operating in a vacuum, it may be a sign that you are doing what you think society approves of, rather than what is right for you. Sycamore shows you how you can give meaning and fulfillment to your life by marching to the beat of your own drummer in your daily activities.

Affirmation

"I act with integrity and concern, according to my own uniqueness, rather than the norms of others."

TULIP TREE

Tulip Poplar, Yellow Poplar
Liriodendron tulipifera

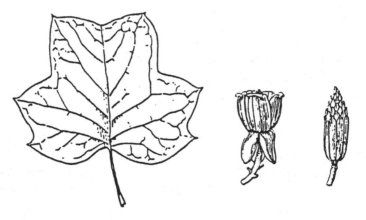

Quality: Redirecting the Emotional Energy of Overindulgence

Physical Aspects

Although this tree is also known as tulip poplar, it is related to the magnolia family, rather than the poplar family. The tulip tree is generally considered to be the tallest tree of the Eastern forest. One reason it looks so tall is because its branches begin very high up, so the trunk seems to soar from the ground right into the sky. The bark is a light gray with uniform ridges.

The tulip tree leaf is easily recognized, with its four lobes and the main vein that ends in a notch. In May and June the tulip tree sheds its large, tulip-like orange and green flowers. The flowers that remain develop into three-inch, cone-like, brown fruits which drop to the ground in the fall.

Tulip Tree Deva

When you have been through an emotionally difficult experience, you may try to detach from it by indulging in food or pleasure beyond moderation. Your excessive indulgence may be an attempt to heal part of you that was hurt in that experience and is seeking love. My energies bring stability to your emotional body so that you can redirect your energies toward healing. I help you to perceive the experience from a more neutral state so that you can move to a space of understanding and balance. Overindulgence is a way of asking for love, and I can help you to give that love to yourself in a manner that leads to more peace inside and a more positive sense of completion from the experience.

Spiritual Aspects

Soul Tone: D
Subtle Body Affinities: Emotional, Spiritual
Element: Water/Earth/Air

Co-creating with Tulip Tree

Tulip tree energy is relaxing, nurturing and centering. It slows you down and creates a space of receptive stability where you can process your experiences and ask for Higher Guidance. When you overindulge in food or other activities in order to avoid emotional pain, tulip tree says, "I will help you create a safe, inner space of nurturing so that you can see what you are feeling and connect with your inner strength and the Light Within. Then you will not need to act from avoidance, but instead you can act with purpose, and moderation." Tulip tree helps you to clarify what you need emotionally, and encourages you to nurture yourself with compassion instead of substances.

Affirmation

"I choose to love myself through moderation, in order to heal emotionally difficult experiences in my life."

BLACK WALNUT

juglans nigra

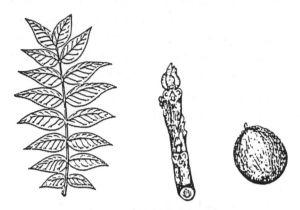

Quality: Speaking About What You Want

Physical Aspects

The large black walnut is more common south of New England and in the Middle West. Before the other leaves fall, black walnut will usually drop its leaves and you can see the large nuts, which grow one to two inches in diameter. These nuts are edible, but cracking the rough shell, with the green spongy husk, is a job.

Black walnut leaves are compound, with fifteen to twenty-three lance-shaped leaflets, each three to four inches long. The end leaflet is usually missing, which is a good identification clue. The crushed leaves give off a spicy scent.

If you slice a thick twig, you will see that it is crossed with partitions, like the ties of a railroad track. The bark is dark brown to gray-black with narrow, rounded ridges.

Black Walnut Deva

My energies teach you that your own level of confidence is not determined by what others think, but what you yourself think. If you allow the doubts of others to affect you, you may feel a fear which lessens your desire to begin and continue new experiences. No one knows better than you whether an experience is right for you. Your own beliefs and attitudes determine the manner in which you learn from an experience. My energies can help you clarify whether what is being said is applicable to your highest interests, or whether it reflects pattens on which the other person is working.

As you move toward a resolution of what you feel and what you want, I support you in expressing from your heart with purity, so that what you say can be assimilated by another with peace. When you express what is in your heart through speaking and through action, you will find that you value and trust yourself more. Your confidence creates an involvement in and a commitment to new growth.

Spiritual Aspects

Soul Tone: E
Subtle Body Affinities: Emotional/Mental
Element: Water/Fire

Co-creating with Black Walnut

Black walnut activates the release of fear or doubt that comes from accepting the imbalanced opinions and feelings of others about a course of action that you wish to take. Its calm, reassuring energy helps you to strengthen your own belief in what is right for you. Sometimes a course of action requires that you go a separate way from another, such as when you move to a new location. Black walnut supports you in communicating what is in your heart to others, so that you can be more at peace with your decisions.

When someone is critical of you, black walnut assists you in holding on to what is important for you, so that you can utilize what is for your highest good, and release all else with equanimity.

Affirmation

"I honor my feelings and my decisions, and I speak from my heart."

BLACK WILLOW

Salix nigra

Quality: Valuing Your Feelings

Physical Aspects

Black willow is the only willow of our over thirty native species that grows into a medium-sized tree. The other natives are generally small trees or shrubs. Walk along any stream bank or other moist location in the eastern United States and you have a good chance of finding black willow.

Black willow leaves are fine-toothed, long and slender, with rounded bases and two tiny, leaf-like appendages at the base of each leaf stem.

The bark of older willows is heavily ridged, swirled and gnarled, with lots of twigs growing out of the knots in the trunk. If these twigs break off into the water, they will root themselves wherever the water floats them ashore. You can easily plant a willow twig by leaving it in a jar of water for several day until its roots sprout, and then planting it in a moist location.

Black willows are especially beautiful in winter because their twigs brighten the landscape with their golden yellow, orange and reddish-brown tints. The buds are covered with a single, reddish-colored bud scale, pressed like sealing wax against the twig.

Black Willow Deva

My gift to the Human Kingdom is to open your sensitivity to your emotional nature so that your emotions can become a powerful tool for healing yourself and others. I work with the pattern where there has been an overemphasis in the attainment of specific goals through the mental energies of your being. When you numb yourself to your emotions, or contend that you are immune to any feelings that would bring pain, you restrict the flow of life-force energy within your being.

I encourage you to value your feelings as a strength, rather than seeing them as a liability. When you can accept rather than judge what you feel, you can then truly release an experience and find ultimate peace with it. You will function as a total and complete being.

Your capacity to help in the healing process of others will also be expanded. When you numb yourself to your own feelings, your ability to understand and empathize with the feelings of others is also impaired, and you may relate to others more on a surface level. Becoming aware of and accepting your own feelings allows you to understand how others feel, and to receive the love that they have to give you.

When you respect the sanctity of your emotional nature and listen to your feelings, you create new gentleness and peace in your life.

Spiritual Aspects

Soul Tone: F
Subtle Body Affinities: Emotional
Element: Water

Co-creating with Black Willow

The willow family strengthens you in integrating your emotional nature into your being. When you are in a space of emotional numbness, black willow urges you to accept that you do have feelings. When this happens you may begin to feel emotional pain, but as you allow yourself to release the pain rather than block it, you will find that you can move through the pain to a place of healing. Black willow reduces the fear involved in this process and keeps you in touch with the Unconditional Love that Lights your way. Its gentle, flowing energy helps you to restore a part of yourself that you have lost, so that you are whole again and living life more fully than ever before.

Affirmation

"I utilize my emotional nature as an ally in my personal growth."

WILLOW OAK

Peach-leaf Oak
Quercus phellos

Quality: Mental Calm

Physical Aspects

Willow oak is essentially a southern tree. It grows from New York to Florida and in the southern states to eastern Texas. You will also find it in the Mississippi Valley as far north as southern Illinois. Look for it on the coastal plain uplands and along stream banks.

Willow oak's leaves are lance-shaped and smooth-edged, like willow leaves. You will notice their leathery texture and the bristle tip, which also appears on each lobe of the red oak. As a member of the oak family, this tree bears small, squat acorns that sit in very shallow, saucer-shaped cups. Its bark is dark and irregularly grooved. Willow oak is nearly evergreen in the southern part of its range, which makes it a delightful shade tree.

Willow Oak Deva

Your mind is a most valuable asset. However, at times when you are inundated with worry, anxiety and repetitive thoughts, your mind acts as a screen that keeps you from sensing fully your own spiritual understanding. My art is one of mentally detaching you from your confusion, and giving you the central focus from a broader perspective. Then your spiritual energies can flow unimpeded into your consciousness, and you can see with clearer insight that which is for your highest good at that moment. The next step is to affirm those emotions and thoughts that are highlighted as important. Then doubt and uncertainty will diminish. My energies teach you how to still your thoughts and center on the purity of your spirit. I also tell you that you have the ability on your own to learn how to become an observer of your reality, after you have experienced this space with me a few times. A key is to allow compassion for yourself to help you build a greater clarity and peace of mind.

Spiritual Aspects

Soul Tone: G#
Subtle Body Affinities: Mental/Spiritual
Element: Air

Co-creating with Willow Oak

If you want to learn how to meditate, willow oak is a fascinating teacher. It can relax your physical body, calm your anxiety, and aid you in releasing thoughts that run in your head like a broken record. Willow oak can create a space in your mind where there is nothing but your existence and the existence of the Spirit. You may notice yourself focusing on your breath, and centering in the present. After you have been in this space for a period of time, you can ask willow oak to help you clarify what is really important. Let it slow you down so that you are better able to open to Greater Understanding and Peace.

Affirmation

"I still my thoughts with compassion, and center on the Purity and Peace of My Spirit."

16 | Ornamental Trees

This chapter describes a few of the many trees that are planted for their beauty, and for food in the case of the apple. We visited two arboretums on our tree travels and were attracted to the trees included in this chapter. We hope that you will explore the qualities of the ornamentals in your area. We begin with two needle-bearing trees, European larch and Norway spruce. Larches, like cypresses, are deciduous and drop their needles in the fall. The broad-leaved trees are then given in alphabetical order.

Trees that are planted in more populated areas give a very special service. It takes more life-force energy for them to maintain themselves, and they give a spiritually stabilizing effect to the environment which is not understood by most people. Take time to touch their leaves and flowers and give them your appreciation and your Unconditional Love for the work that they do.

EUROPEAN LARCH

Larix decidua

Quality: Creative Expansion

Physical Aspects

The European larch has been so widely planted that it is perhaps the most common larch in the northeastern United States. In its native Europe, it thrives in cool, mountainous regions north to the Arctic circle. In this country it enjoys the upland areas. American larch or tamarack grows in swamps and bogs, and so one way to distinguish the two species is by location.

European larch needles are one-and-one-quarter inches long, longer than American larch. They grow in bunches of eighteen or more, on short spurs. The larch family is one of the few conifer families that sheds its needles in the fall, after they turn yellow. In winter, the one-quarter-inch-long spurs give the branches a coarse, lumpy appearance. European larch branchlets droop, and its cones are about one inch long, unlike American larch whose cones are one-half-inch long. These cones remain upright on the tree, and are often attached for several years after they mature. The red-brown trunk is relatively smooth when the tree is young, and then becomes divided into large platelets.

European Larch Deva

I expand your vision of your potential, so that you can find even more dynamic ways of working with your skills in a creative manner. When you say, ''This is all I can do,'' or "I can't move into a new area because I don't know enough," my energies support you in believing in yourself. Change is a necessary part of growth, and there is a time in your personal growth cycle for expanding beyond where you have been. The greatest gift that you can give to yourself is to become more aware of the possibilities that are present for you and to take action. You are then choosing to grow into a stronger and more confident being. Open to your spiritual nature and allow your creative expression to marry the spiritual and physical realities as you perceive them. Then you will also express a broader picture of Who You Truly Are.

Spiritual Aspects

Soul Tone: C
Subtle Body Affinities: Emotional/Mental
Element: Fire

Co-creating with Larch

European larch is one of the confidence builders, broadening your vision of who you can be. For example, if you are a trim carpenter and you are attracted to European larch, perhaps you are being told that it is time to expand your creative potential. Larch heightens your enthusiasm for new possibilities. Starting your own business, cabinetry or creative woodworking may suddenly seem appealing and distinctly possible to execute. European larch aids you in dissolving a narrowness of vision, fear or self-doubt, so that you can bring your dreams into reality with confidence and excitement.

Affirmation

"I expand my vision of what I can do and bring my dreams into reality."

NORWAY SPRUCE

Picea abies

Quality: Dedication

Physical Aspects

Norway spruce is a large, European species that has become a naturalized member of our forests and is extensively planted as an ornamental. Its bottom branches sweep out close to the ground, while its top reaches skyward like a steeple, giving this tree a uniform, conical shape.

Like other spruces, its needles are sharp, four-sided, and they grow all around the twigs. When the needles are removed, the twigs remain rough. Norway spruce needles are about three-quarters of an inch long.

A distinctive characteristic of this spruce is the way its branchlets droop. Norway spruce cones are four inches long, longer than other Eastern spruce cones.

Norway Spruce Deva

You have heard it said that one of your important lessons is living your truth by allowing your way of life to reflect your spiritual nature. At this time in the evolution of humankind, there is a need to integrate more spiritual understanding with your everyday Earth plane reality.

My energies intensify the concentration of your spiritual energies into your daily affairs. I encourage you to become more involved in daily spiritual practices that are comfortable, and which bring you into a state of peace and centeredness. It is important not to force yourself in any way to work with a particular tool, so that you are not restricted from receiving its positive benefits. If you are feeling highly agitated at the time you choose to work with your practice, utilize it to help you regain your balance, and then work with the practice at another time where you will be more receptive to its higher frequencies. Honor your own personal rhythms and pause when you need to receive something in the moment. In these ways you can bring spiritual understanding through daily activities into your physical reality.

My energies reflect the sanctity of the heart, and the quality of dedication. The more that you strengthen the connection between your spiritual reality and your daily activities, the stronger you will become in service to the Planet.

Spiritual Aspects

Soul Tone: C
Subtle Body Affinities: Emotional/Mental
Element: Earth/Fire

Co-creating with Norway Spruce

Norway spruce strengthens your concentration and dedication to your spiritual path. If you are unsure about ways to deepen your spiritual connection, Norway spruce can help you find an appropriate path for your current space. If you feel as though you have been drifting, and empty, or living on the surface of things, Norway spruce elevates your desire to find out how you can express your gifts in service to others.

Affirmation

"I strengthen my commitment and my dedication to integrate my spiritual knowing into my everyday reality."

APPLE

Malus pumila domestica

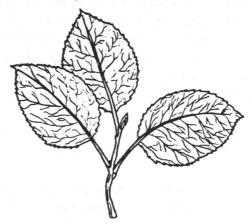

Quality: Fear and Abundance

Physical Aspects

Apples have been a favorite fruit for thousands of years. Scientists studying the ruins of Stone Age villages in Europe have found the charcoal remains of apples. The Greeks were known to grow several varieties of apples, and the Romans spread various kinds of apples throughout Europe during their military conquests.

Edible varieties of apples are improved by grafting the wood from preferred trees onto native rootstock. The original Baldwin tree, for example, was discovered by Baldwin in 1793 in a corner of his property in Lowell, Massachusetts. If you plant a hybrid apple seed, the resulting tree reverts to its original wild state, so it is only through grafting that a consistent quality is maintained.

You may associate apples with Johnny Appleseed, which was the name given to John Chapman (1774–1845). From about 1800 until his death he traveled alone from western Pennsylvania through Ohio, Indiana, and Illinois, planting orchards and distributing apple seeds and saplings to settlers moving westward. He became a legendary figure for a number of reasons. His appearance was eccentric, as his usual dress was an old coffee sack shirt, ragged trousers, bare feet, and an inverted mush pan for a hat. He was devoted to the Bible and quoted it often to anyone who would listen. The native Americans respected him as a medicine man because of his gentleness with animals and his knowledge of medicinal herbs. By the time

of his death, he had planted about twelve hundred acres of apple orchards and encouraged others to plant apple trees as well.

An apple leaf is roundly oval, with toothed edges and soft,
woolly hair on the underside, and also on the long-leaf stem. The
flowers open just after the leaves, with five pink petals that turn
white. These flowers grow in clusters and produce abundant nectar,
which attracts bees. The twigs which support the apples are blunt-
tipped and stubby, like a compressed screen door swing. Many a
youngster has sat on the sturdy branches of this tree with its gray
bark and gnarled, spiraling ridges, while enjoying an apple.

Apple Deva

It is very important when you are on the Earth Plane
to develop the ability to recognize when feelings and
thoughts are affecting your physical body. When your
thoughts involve anger, irritation or bitterness, the pattern
of imbalance can significantly reduce the flow of life-force
energy in your physical body. You may then experience increased toxins, or conditions of ''stuck'' energy such as
constipation or congestion of some kind. When you have
a physical imbalance, I ask you to assess what you are
thinking and feeling because if you treat only the physical
symptoms and not what is happening with your thoughts,
the symptoms will return in the same form or in other
forms.

Many conditions and feelings of anger and bitterness
result from a fear of lack, or feeling that something is missing in your life. You may feel that nothing will change and
your resources will be taken away in some manner. I tell
you to value the resources in your midst so that when you
affirm the abundance present, you become open for additional resources to come into your life.

Do not underestimate the effect that the spiritual com-
ponent of your being can have on your present state of affairs. Within the spiritual realm, all can be manifested, and
you can trust that what you affirm is taking place. If you do
not feel worthy to receive certain things, the way for them
to come to you will be blocked, as you yourself have so
deemed it. Allow yourself to trust in the positive outcome

of your experiences and feel the support that is with you. In this way you can release physical congestion and toxicity, and create more energy flow in your life.

Spiritual Aspects

Soul Tone: D#
Subtle Body Affinities: Emotional/Mental
Element: Water

Co-creating with Apple

Apples are considered to be healthy for your physical body, and the spiritual qualities of apple relate to promoting your physical health by identifying and releasing fearful thoughts that cause congestion and blockage. If you feel stuck in fear, you can shelter in the warmth and comfort of apple, which increases your ability to focus on what is abundant and right in your life. Apple is both cleansing and nurturing, asking you to listen to what your body needs, and to flow with the river of life, rather than holding onto the rocks.

Affirmation

"I listen to my body, and release fear through trusting in the abundance of life."

GINGKO

Maidenhair Tree
Gingko biloba

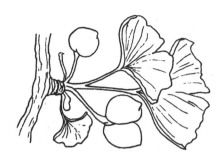

Quality: Androgyny

Physical Aspects

The gingko tree is the only remaining representative of the oldest living species of tree, dating back two hundred million years to the time of the dinosaurs. The name "gingko" is derived from the Japanese name for the white seed kernels, which are considered a delicacy in the East. It is believed to be a native of northern China where Chinese Buddhist monks cultivated these trees in order to save them from extinction. The gingko has been revered by the Chinese for its longevity, and some trees are believed to be more than one thousand years old. The gingko is known today as one of the most disease- and pollution-resistant trees in the world, and it thrives cheerfully along our city streets.

No other leaf looks like a gingko leaf, which is one- or two-lobed and fan-shaped. The leaf blade is attached by a rather long stalk to the twig. In the fall the leaves turn a brilliant yellow.

Gingkos produce separate male and female trees. The male tree bears a pollen-bearing cone. The pollen swims like fern sperms, through rain or dew, instead of being blown or transported by insects. It is believed that this is a primitive feature that has been maintained from the dinosaur times. It takes thirty years before the berry-like seeds are produced. The outer husk of the mature seed has a distinctive odor that some find offensive, and for this reason, it is usually the male trees that are planted ornamentally.

Gingko Deva

More and more Light is ushering forth onto your Planet as each of you works to change your consciousness. There is to be a bonding of the male and female energies, and as this happens, you are going to witness more people speaking out from an androgynous way of being. Because my species has been on the earth plane for a very long time, my male and female energies have become very refined. I represent a male or female form as you do, but my male and female energies are bonded. Therefore, I can assist in the realignment of your male and female polarities so that you can act from the balanced state of androgyny.

You choose a male or female vehicle in order to develop the qualities of that polarity. If you are male you are purifying your will towards actions that bring a more positive quality of life to others. If you are female you are developing the qualities of receptivity and sensitivity that bring Oneness to your relationships with others. The opposite vehicle represents areas of your growth that you have developed in other lifetimes, and you can call upon the gifts of your opposite polarity to assist you in your current lifetime.

Even though you are born in a male or female body, you contain both masculine and feminine energies within you. The goal is to seek the outward expression and creative use of both of these frequencies within self, rather than to express predominantly the masculine or the feminine energies. Those who live longer lives are those beings who know how to balance both energies. If you express only your masculine energies, you may find yourself living at an accelerated pace that can lead to a breakdown in functioning. If you express only your feminine energies you may find yourself reluctant to use your will in making the choices that you need to make. Your choices ultimately determine how long your physical vehicle is available to you.

I can help you examine the beliefs that you may have adopted about yourself as a man or a woman, and support you in moving toward balance in your personal growth. What is needed is openness, faith and trust in your unfoldment. When you live in Oneness with your male and female energies, you have a greater acceptance of all forms of life and how they manifest in the world.

Spiritual Aspects

Soul Tone: B
Subtle Body Affinities: Emotional/Mental, Spiritual
Element: Air

Co-creating with Gingko

You can work with gingko by asking, "How do I need to develop the male side of me?" and "How do I need to develop the female side of me?" Gingko can create a vision of what the androgynous you is like, and will leave you in a space of peace and centered balance.

Affirmation

"I express the perfect blend of feminine and masculine energies through my chosen physical vehicle."

SOUTHERN MAGNOLIA

Bull Bay
Magnolia grandiflora

Quality: Making Difficult Choices

Physical Aspects

Magnolia grows naturally in the moist, fertile soils of the southeastern Atlantic coast and the Gulf coast, but it is widely planted ornamentally. Everything about this tree is lush. The ever-green leaves are dark green, waxy ovals with rusty undersides. They are so prolific that the shade under them is cool and dark. When you look at the large flowers, you might think of creamy white water lilies. The air around a magnolia in summer is redolent with the distinct, sweet fragrance of these flowers.

Southern Magnolia Deva

You seek to comprehend the totality of your experiences; however, quite often what you seek to know is veiled to an extent, so that you can learn the most from a particular experience. When you feel resistant to an ongoing situation, I help you through my energies to trust your inner sense of knowing the appropriate response. Sometimes this means choosing to continue the experience because something positive is being gained, or sometimes it means to disengage from the experience.

A difficult space may be meant to strengthen you, and to teach you qualities of attention, and discipline. It may be necessary to undergo a situation so that you can better expand the awareness of others in their own growth with this experience. You may have to let go of an immediate sense of fulfillment with an activity in order to have an even greater fulfillment take place later in life. You develop more facets of your being as you work with activities that test your determination, as well as with those experiences that are easy and flowing. I can support you in working with greater acceptance and peace in your space, so that you can achieve the most positive interchange that you can.

A significant struggle with an experience may also indicate its incompatibility with your present needs. You may then choose to disconnect from a situation because of its imbalancing effect upon your life-force energies. It is vital that you not judge your decision in any manner, or the very pattern from which you are seeking to free yourself will remain in your space. I tell you to be thankful for what has been. Learning comes in many forms, and there will be many opportunities for you to learn what you need for your growth. Your overall objective is to value yourself in all experiences and to continue to serve your Highest Good.

Spiritual Aspects

Soul Tone: E
Subtle Body Affinities: Emotional/Mental
Element: Air

Co-creating with Southern Magnolia

Southern magnolia assists you in coming to a decision about an unpleasant experience, and to accept your choice with compassion. Sometimes it is easy to complain or despair about an experience, and assume that you are inevitably stuck in it. You just suffer along and "put up" with the situation without learning from it. Southern magnolia urges you to make a choice and get on with your life, with increased understanding about the lessons that you are learning.

Affirmation

"I make the decision to live more consciously, understanding the lessons of my current situation, or choosing to change."

WEEPING WILLOW
Salix babylonica

Quality: Moving Through the Grief Process

Physical Aspects

Weeping willow is an old-world tree that was planted by the original settlers from Europe, and it is widely planted today as an ornamental. Its twigs are extremely long and droopy, and the whole tree has a soft, flexible appearance.

Weeping willow leaves are very thin, often silky, and whitened beneath. Like black willow, weeping willow has golden yellow-green twigs that make this tree stand out in the winter. For many of us the budding weeping willow leaves are one of the first signs of spring.

Weeping Willow Deva

When there has been a crisis of loss, sometimes an emotional numbness sets in because the feelings are too painful. I tell you that you must look at what has occurred and feel what needs to be felt, so that you can have the freedom of greater peace inside your being.

If you are physically separated from someone you love through death or transition, trying to avoid the pain of that loss will also suppress the memories of the positive qualities of that person that can heal you.

Contained within any loss is a positive value, a support that can help you move through pain. I can help you find the inner strength and the Light with which to heal.

You can learn much about flexibility from my twigs and branchlets. I teach you to move with life rather than resist what you are feeling. When one of my branches becomes disconnected, it will grow into a new tree if it is planted in some soil. You are both the disconnected branch and the old tree, and contained within you is the capacity for growth and healing wherever you are.

I can also teach you how to give to someone close to you who has suffered a loss. It does not help the griever for you to relate a similar experience, because that keeps the griever focused in his or her own loss. The greatest gift you have to give is your capacity to listen with compassion and understanding. It is a sacred honor and trust to be a spiritual catalyst in another person's healing, and when you Unconditionally Love another, you facilitate your own healing as well.

Spiritual Aspects

Soul Tone: F
Subtle Body Affinities: Emotional
Element: Water

Co-creating with Weeping Willow

The willow family reconnects you with your feeling nature. Weeping willow energy can ease emotional numbness during the crisis of loss. It encourages healing tears and supports you in moving through the necessary stages of grieving. This tree is certainly aptly named, and can teach you much about allowing and flowing with the healing process rather than fighting it.

Affirmation

"Light is always supporting me in my grief."

PART THREE

The Healing Tree—
Co-creating for Personal and
Planetary Healing

In Part Three we have included two final chapters to aid you in co-creating with trees for personal and planetary healing. Chapter seventeen summarizes the tree qualities and organizes the trees according to family, rather than by region. The particular focus or quality of the tree, the specific imbalance it helps to correct, as well as an affirmation that expresses the tree's energy are included under each entry. You can use this material in several ways. If you are feeling a particular imbalance, you might check the summaries for the trees in your area, to see which tree qualities might be most helpful. As we stated earlier in chapter seven, it can be valuable to affirm the overall quality of a family, even if you do not know the identity of a particular tree. Also, when you are in the presence of several trees of the same species, you can go to the tree which gives the specific qualities that you need. Our own understanding of tree qualities was strengthened as we noticed the similarities and differences of trees from various parts of the country. We have thus summarized our perceptions in order to provide you with additional clarity.

Chapter eighteen provides answers to questions we have asked the Devas about co-creating with trees for healing, as well as material that the Devas themselves wished us to record. This final chapter is like a seed that contains an ending as well as a beginning. We and the Devas wish you to plant the seeds of change which you have received through your commitment to more deeply understand the Kingdoms of Nature, and to help others to grow in Unconditional Love.

17 | Summary of Tree Qualities by Family

Alder, Red Joy
> *Focus:* Increases joy and enthusiasm in the present moment.
> *Imbalance:* Living in the past rather than the present, depression, pessimism.
> *Affirmation:* "The power in being lies in seeking the newness of each moment."

Apple Fear and Abundance
> *Focus:* Activates the warmth and comfort of knowing that you are supported by the abundance of the universe.
> *Imbalance:* Fear of lack or emptiness, that causes congestion in the physical body.
> *Affirmation:* "I listen to my body, and release fear through trusting in the abundance of life."

Ash, White Clarification of Values
> *Focus:* Detaches you from your emotions so that you can clarify your values and assess what you really believe.
> *Imbalance:* Confusion about what you really want for yourself, being overly affected by what others believe, untested assumptions about the course of your life.
> *Affirmation:* "I open my mind to my spiritual nature in order to clarify my beliefs and make clear decisions."

Aspen, Quaking   **Moving from Anxiety to Opportunity**
Focus: Heightens a sense of safety and anticipation for what is to come, so that you can see more possibilities for growth.
Imbalance: Fear, worry or anxiety about a future experience.
Affirmation: "Fear becomes an opportunity, as I affirm safety in opening to new possibilities for growth."

Beech   **Tolerance**
Focus: Strengthens tolerance and compassion for others as you choose through your own will the quality of growth that you seek for yourself.
Imbalance: Intolerance, difficulty in seeing how an experience connects with learning to love more deeply.
Affirmation: "I affirm that many paths lead to Wisdom, and I treat others with tolerance and understanding."

BIRCH   Better Understanding and Healing in Relationships

River Birch   **Risking in Relationships**
Focus: Strengthens trust in initiating new relationships.
Imbalance: Fear of rejection, an increased sense of vulnerability, hesitancy.
Affirmation: "I now risk opening myself to a new relationship, trusting that I am being supported in this experience."

Yellow Birch   **Acceptance of Others in Relationships**
Focus: Increases tolerance, and the desire to get to know the real person.
Imbalance: Stereotyping others, seeing oneself as separate from others.
Affirmation: "In relationships, I accept others for who they are without judgment, as I wish to be accepted."

Black Birch   **Confronting Self in Relationships**
Focus: Activates the desire to examine your own emotions and behavior in a relationship more deeply.
Imbalance: Tendency to blame the other for problems in a relationship. Focusing on superficial disagreements rather than the underlying conflicts.
Affirmation: "I open to what I need to learn in order to build a stronger intimate relationship."

Paper Birch   **Reconciliation in Relationships**
Focus: Increases empathy for others, and the willingness to see another's point of view. Aids in finding the common ground that brings you together.
Imbalance: Pride that keeps you from seeing another's point of view, difficulty accepting what is right for another person, lack of empathy.
Affirmation: "I seek greater awareness, trust and harmony in all my relationships."

Gray Birch   **Separation in Relationships**
Focus: Assists you in knowing when a learning in a relationship is complete, and the relationship needs to take a different form.
Imbalance: Reluctance and difficulty in taking the responsibility to initiate change.
Affirmation: "I am healed by focusing on the positive nature of what I am learning in all stages of my relationships."

Box Elder   **Spiritual Expansion**
Focus: Brings into focus the broader spiritual meaning of an experience, connects you with your Higher Self.
Imbalance: Fear of connecting with your spiritual nature, difficulty in deepening your meditation.
Affirmation: "I open to my spiritual nature, in order to seek that which is for my Highest Good."

Buckeye, Ohio   **Learning and Letting Go**
Focus: Cheers you on to take events in your stride with your sense of self intact, so that you can let an experience go.
Imbalance: Difficulty putting an experience in perspective, oversensitivity to criticism, lack of assertiveness.
Affirmation: "I learn from an experience through believing in myself and not looking back."

CEDAR   Aligning Your Personal Will with Your Highest Good

Eastern Red Cedar   **Courage**
Focus: Builds confidence and certainty that you can pursue your goals.
Imbalance: Self-doubt, anxiety and fear of the unknown.
Affirmation: "I courageously embrace the unknown and acknowledge every choice as a learning experience."

Western Red Cedar   Self-determination

Focus: Activates your inner strength and determination to move ahead, regardless of the opinions of others.

Imbalance: Feelings of restriction, frustration or reluctance to take action, caused by allowing yourself to be excessively influenced by the opinions of others.

Affirmation: "My own inner strength guides me, and my next step becomes clear, as I release the influence of others in determining my actions."

Incense Cedar   Purifying the Will

Focus: Activates you to purify and redirect your will, opening to the Highest Good for all concerned.

Imbalance: Anger when your desires are thwarted, trying to establish power or control over others.

Affirmation: "I act according to the Highest Good for all concerned."

COTTONWOOD   Being in the Present with Your Physical Body

Eastern Cottonwood   Honoring Your Physical Body

Focus: Assists you in honoring your physical body and listening to its needs, developing a more intuitive connection with your body.

Imbalance: Viewing your body as unimportant and ignoring its messages.

Affirmation: "I live harmoniously within self, by honoring my body, mind and spirit."

Black Cottonwood   Bringing Spirit into Body

Focus: Affirms the rightness of your physical vehicle for the lessons you have come to learn, and the service that you give.

Imbalance: Judging the limitations of your physical body.

Affirmation: "My physical body is a mirror of my Divine Essence."

Cypress, Bald   Outer and Inner Security

Focus: Builds security in your own inner resources, so that you live with a sense of safety and abundance.

Imbalance: Insecurity and worry about lack in your life.

Affirmation: "I am centered in the security and abundance of my own power."

Dogwood, Flowering   **Seeing Beauty in All Things**
Focus: Heightens your aesthetic appreciation of your environment, enables you to seek the healing beauty in others.
Imbalance: Insensitivity to beauty, numbness caused by inner pain.
Affirmation: "I honor the beauty that is all around me, as well as my own beauty."

Douglas Fir   **Honoring Your Gifts**
Focus: Supports the honoring of the gifts and qualities that you bring to the world, so that you recognize inside yourself who you are.
Imbalance: Belittling self, feeling insignificant, looking outside self for definition.
Affirmation: "I stand tall and honor my gifts with a spiritual sense of self."

Elm, American   **Compassionate Self-honesty**
Focus: Assists you in seeking a balance between giving to others and caring for your own personal needs.
Imbalance: Devaluing your own needs, by placing the needs of others before your own.
Affirmation: "I am honest with myself about who I am, what my needs are, and what I can do."

Eucalyptus   **Increasing Your Physical Vitality**
Focus: Valuing your physical body, becoming more aware of its needs, and increasing your physical vitality through attention to your breath.
Imbalance: Ignoring your body, stressing your body through shallow breathing.
Affirmation: "I listen to the messages that my physical body is giving me, and I connect with body through my breath."

FIR   Bringing Subconscious Beliefs into Conscious Awareness

California Red Fir   **Clearing Subconscious Memories in Adults**
Focus: Activates the release of past life memories and other subconscious memories in adults.
Imbalance: Emotional and mental pain from subconscious memories that are affecting the present.
Affirmation: "I now release subconscious memories, and I fill my being with Love."

White Fir　Clearing Subconscious Memories in Children
Focus: Activates the release of past life memories and other subconscious memories in children.
Imbalance: Emotional and mental pain, from subconscious memories in childern, that affects the present.
Affirmation: "White Fir, you are my special friend."

Grand Fir　Becoming Aware of Subconscious Emotional Wounds
Focus: Increases awareness of the causes of emotional pain from earlier years in your present life, and promotes release of these subconscious memories.
Imbalance: Difficulty in understanding what is emotionally upsetting to you, when the cause lies in the experience of your earlier years.
Affirmation: "I choose now to become aware of and to release old burdens."

Pacific Silver Fir　Releasing Current Emotional Upsets
Focus: Understanding and releasing emotions of the immediate moment, relating to your daily activities.
Imbalance: Rationalizing or ignoring feelings for which at least some of the cause is apparent.
Affirmation: "I am filled with peace and Unconditional Love, as I release upsets from each new day."

Gingko　Androgyny
Focus: Promotes balance of the masculine and feminine energies inside self.
Imbalance: Neglecting the masculine or feminine parts of self that need to be developed.
Affirmation: "I express the perfect balance of feminine and masculine energies through my chosen physical vehicle."

HEMLOCK　Developing Faith through Trusting the Process of Change

Eastern Hemlock　Openness to Change
Focus: Accepting change in your life with trust, and focusing on the present moment.
Imbalance: Complacency, trying to hold onto old ways that have become inappropriate for the present.

Affirmation: "I choose to open to the new opportunities in my changing circumstances."

Western Hemlock   Faith
Focus: Supports your faith in the face of difficult circumstances, letting you know that change means that all experiences pass.
Imbalance: Incapacitation because you feel like a victim.
Affirmation: "My faith increases as I trust the Light."

HICKORY   Clarifying and Prioritizing Your Thinking

Shellbark Hickory   Mental Focus
Focus: Activates your ability to prioritize your thoughts so that you can complete your task.
Imbalance: Acting impulsively and scattering your energies, difficulty in completing tasks.
Affirmation: "I prioritize my thoughts, in order to maintain my focus and complete my tasks."

Shagbark Hickory   Organizing with Enthusiasm
Focus: Increases involvement and enthusiasm with the process of organizing your thoughts and completing your tasks.
Imbalance: Lack of interest or boredom with your tasks so that they remain uncompleted, acting without purpose.
Affirmation: "I enthusiastically express my mental wisdom."

Pignut Hickory   Timely Manifestation
Focus: Heightens your sense of timing for when to plan and when to act.
Imbalance: Drifting, procrastinating or rushing headlong into action without adequate planning.
Affirmation: "I listen to my inner direction on when it is time to wait and plan, and when it is time to act."

Larch   Creative Expansion
Focus: Expands your vision of who you can be and what you can create.
Imbalance: Narrowness of vision, lack of confidence.
Affirmation: "I expand my vision of what I can do and bring my dreams into reality."

Live Oak, Coast   Conscious Assimilation of Experience
Focus: Encourages you to take the time and space in your life to integrate your experiences.

Imbalance: Valuing busyness, filling your schedule too full, looking to the future for fulfillment.

Affirmation: "I discern what is essential for me to be doing, and I appreciate everything that I do more fully."

Locust, Black   Assessment without Judgment

Focus: Supports you in taking responsibility for your actions without blaming self or others.

Imbalance: Refusing to take responsibility for your actions, blaming others, blaming self.

Affirmation: "I assess my actions without judgment, and I take responsibility for them, without blaming others."

Madrone, Pacific   Stewardship

Focus: Activates the wise use of your material resources, and the practical use of your time and energy.

Imbalance: Wastefulness, overextending your time and energy.

Affirmation: "I release any imbalance that clutters my knowing of what I truly need present in my life."

Magnolia, Southern   Making Difficult Choices

Focus: Assists you in seeing how your daily activities support your growth, and broadens your confidence in seeking something more.

Imbalance: Assuming that you are stuck in your current situation, drifting along without understanding your purpose with a particular activity.

Affirmation: "I make the decision to live more consciously, understanding the lessons of my current situation, or choosing to change."

MAPLE   Giving and Receiving Unconditional Love

Red Maple   Enjoying Your Unique Self

Focus: Activates the desire to reach out to others, by heightening your understanding of what you have to give.

Imbalance: Shyness, reticence, avoiding others because you have been hurt.

Affirmation: "I share my special Light with others, and enjoy my expansion."

Sugar Maple   Affirming Others

Focus: Mirroring to others their special, beautiful qualities.

Imbalance: Disappointment or frustration with others, being overly critical of others.

Affirmation: "I honor you and I rejoice in your special gifts."

Silver Maple   Healing Disappointment in Relationships

Focus: Assists you in affirming the positive qualities of another, and your own gifts to the relationship, during times of separation.

Imbalance: Disappointment or disillusionment with another, loneliness.

Affirmation: "Your Light is always with me, showing me my path toward Unconditional Love and Inner Peace."

Bigleaf Maple   Interconnectedness with All of Life

Focus: Inspires a broader perspective on what you give and receive from others, and on the companionship that Nature can give.

Imbalance: Feeling separate from others, disappointment with others, loneliness, difficulty enjoying pleasure.

Affirmation: "I learn to give and receive Unconditional Love so that others know the presence of that Divine Love within themselves."

OAK   Developing the Strength of Your Inner Resources

White Oak   Steadfast Stength

Focus: Enables you to accept and develop the current space and time in your life with a patient, stable strength.

Imbalance: Impatience, discontent with where you are at the moment.

Affirmation: "I flow with my current opportunities and accept what is."

Red Oak   Resourcefulness

Focus: Increases your resourcefulness in your present situation.

Imbalance: Pessimism and impatience that come from a desire to be moving on.

Affirmation: "I flow with my current space and explore my resources more fully."

Chestnut Oak   Focusing on the Present

Focus: Accepting a change in your resources, and integrating past resources into your present space.

Imbalance: Regretting the past that leads to despondency, lethargy, pessimism.

Affirmation: "I integrate into the present the resources that I have developed in the past, so that I can create from a strong, inner center."

Mossycup Oak   Continuity through Integration

Focus: Facilitates the mental evaluation of where you are going so that you can develop your inner resources with purpose.

Imbalance: Fear, hesitation, confusion about how your present space integrates with your future.

Affirmation: "I integrate my personal resources in order to provide a continuity between my present and future actions."

Pin Oak   Hope

Focus: Valuing your inner resources in light of what you are contributing to the greater good.

Imbalance: Discontentment or discouragement about your present space.

Affirmation: "I value my inner resources and the contributions I am making to the greater good."

Valley Oak   Fulfillment

Focus: Inspires a more complete sense of spiritual fulfillment in the difficult work of developing your inner resources.

Imbalance: Emptiness, feeling that what you do is never quite enough, difficulty in giving yourself recognition for your own inner strength.

Affirmation: "My fulfillment comes from honoring the strength and wisdom that I am creating inside me."

PINE   Releasing Self-criticism and Unrealistic Expectations of Self

Eastern White Pine   Becoming Aware of Self-Judgment

Focus: Activates a greater awareness of self-critical attitudes and unrealistic expectations.

Imbalance: Anger, depression or low energy due to self-judgment and unnecessary standards or goals.

Affirmation: "I acknowledge who I am as a lovable and capable person."

Loblolly Pine   **Emotional Equanimity**
Focus: Calms and centers you so that you can release guilt and self-judgment.
Imbalance: Emotional agitation, worry, and fear, caused by difficulty in releasing self-critical attitudes about an experience.
Affirmation: "I regain my emotional balance so that I can let go of self-judgment and choose clearly how to affirm myself."

Sugar Pine   **Emotional Empathy**
Focus: Increases your ability to understand and accept different parts of yourself.
Imbalance: Self-blame, judging your inner child.
Affirmation: "I accept the needs of my inner child."

Jeffrey Pine   **Versatility**
Focus: Adjusting your standards so that your goals include a greater acceptance of what you need to learn. Promotes a greater versatility in thinking.
Imbalance: Limiting yourself by setting expectations that are too narrow or rigid. Inflexibility in thinking about your own standards and goals.
Affirmation: "I am following my direction with a versatile tolerance that affirms who I am in the present moment."

Lodgepole Pine   **Resilience**
Focus: Aids in the releasing of self-condemnation related to the loss of purpose. Motivates you toward a particular goal.
Imbalance: Despondency, despair, loss of goal direction.
Affirmation: "I tenaciously hold to my path, reassured that I am moving closer to Greater Light."

Ponderosa Pine   **Foregiveness**
Focus: Increases the serenity of mind that comes from forgiving self.
Imbalance: Self-blame, inability to forgive self.
Affirmation: "I accept myself as I am, and I forgive myself and others."

SEQUOIA   **Triumphing over Life's Adversities**

Coastal Redwood   **The Inspiration of Transcendence**
Focus: Inspires you to believe in a Plan or a Pattern greater than yourself.

Imbalance: Feeling insignificant or defeated, fear that death is the absolute end of life.
Affirmation: "I merge with Unconditional Love, to become Greater than myself."

Giant Sequoia　The Mastery of Transcendence
Focus: Supports your will to be and to survive.
Imbalance: Desire to give up, discouragement, fear of death as the absolute end of life.
Affirmation: "The Unconditional Love of God transcends all human conditions and experiences."

SPRUCE　Strengthening Your Commitment to Your Spiritual Purpose in Life

Norway Spruce　Dedication
Focus: Strengthens the concentration of your spiritual energies into your daily affairs.
Imbalance: Emptiness, reluctance or lack of discipline in committing yourself to spiritual attitudes and practices.
Affirmation: "I strengthen my commitment and dedication to integrate my spiritual knowing into my everyday reality."

Red Spruce　Integrating the Past with Your Spiritual Purpose
Focus: Assists you in finding the meaning of your past experiences in fulfilling your spiritual purpose.
Imbalance: Seeing past experiences as meaningless, feeling as though your life is a series of random events.
Affirmation: "I understand how the experiences of the past have contributed to my spiritual growth and purpose in this life."

Sitka Spruce　Understanding Your Spiritual Purpose
Focus: Gives a deeper awareness of your spiritual purpose, affirms your steps in the process of fulfilling that purpose.
Imbalance: Discouragement or disillusionment about whether you are truly on your spiritual path.
Affirmation: "My inner guidance reassures me that I am fulfilling my spiritual purpose."

Blue Spruce　Peace
Focus: Embracing your physical reality with greater stewardship and becoming a more active mirror for others.

Imbalance: Lack of fulfillment in what you are accomplishing.
Affirmation: "Everything that I share with others is born from the Inner Peace within me."

Englemann Spruce The Joy of Fulfillment

Focus: Increases your capacity for deeper joy and appreciation of self and others as you fulfill your spiritual purpose.
Imbalance: Dedication without joy, seeing various aspects of your life as unrelated.
Affirmation: "I am now expressing my spiritual essence on all levels of my being."

Sweetgum Initiative, Involvement, Completion

Focus: Heightens involvement with a process, and the desire to complete what you have started.
Imbalance: Ambivalance or a lack or interest in your activities, procrastination.
Affirmation: "My time is now, and I start and finish my activities with deeper enthusiasm and involvement."

Sycamore Concern for the Quality of All Life

Focus: Creating a more caring environment for others in everything that you do, listening to your own heart about what is right to do.
Imbalance: Doing what others do even when it goes against your personal beliefs, a sense of stagnation or a lack of fulfillment in life.
Affirmation: "I act with integrity and concern, according to my own uniqueness rather than the norms of others."

Tulip Tree Redirecting the Emotional Energy of Overindulgence

Focus: Creates a space of receptive stability that enables you to examine why you are overindulging. Aids you in acting with moderation.
Imbalance: Overindulging, avoiding dealing with pain, acting in excess.
Affirmation: "I choose to love myself through moderation, in order to heal emotionally difficult experiences in my life."

Black Walnut Speaking About What You Want

Focus: Strengthens your belief about what is right for you and enables you to speak to others from your heart.

Imbalance: Being overly influenced by the opinions of others, fear and hesitancy about speaking out.
Affirmation: "I honor my feelings and my decisions, and I speak from my heart."

WILLOW   Opening to Your Emotional Nature

Black Willow   Valuing Your Feelings

Focus: Valuing your feelings, increasing your sensitivity to others, respecting the role that emotions play in the healing process.
Imbalance: Ignoring, or numbing yourself to your feelings, insensitivity to the feelings of others.
Affirmation: "I utilize my emotional nature as an ally in my personal growth."

Weeping Willow   Moving through the Grief Process

Focus: Supports you in feelings of loss so that you can heal your grief.
Imbalance: Emotional numbness during the crisis of loss, avoiding the feelings of grief.
Affirmation: "Light is always supporting me in my grief."

Willow Oak   Mental Calm

Focus: Creates a calm space in your mind where you can hear Spirit, centers you in the present.
Imbalance: Scattered thoughts, inability to focus mentally, difficulty in connecting with your Higher Guidance.
Affirmation: "I still my thoughts with compassion, and center on the Purity and Peace of My Spirit."

18 | Co-creating with Nature to Heal Our Environment

PERSONAL AND PLANETARY healing are connected, as the Douglas Fir Deva explains:

> When you love yourself, we can focus the life-force energy of your positive thoughts and feelings to life species and to places on the planet that are in need of healing. Fear diminishes life-force energy. Love amplifies it. As you learn to love yourself through your thoughts and actions, you assist in the evolution of Consciousness in the Human Kingdom.
>
> When you live in a state of love you have the capacity to co-create with us because an aspect of loving is focusing on the highest good for all forms of life. If you keep your thoughts focused on the overall balance of life on this planet, you will be guided in the actions you can take in your personal space.

This chapter continues the teachings we have received from the Devas, particularly on how we can work more closely with Nature to heal our environment.

SPIRITUAL GROWTH THROUGH COMMUNICATION AND COOPERATION

When you are living on the earth and you focus primarily on meeting the basic needs of your physical existence, you are living through your body, mind and feelings. When you affirm through your words and actions that you want to open to your spiritual essence, you awaken your greater spiritual potential to the Light. You can then be with us, through your sense of Oneness with All That Is. We come to serve because we learn through our giving on behalf of other lifestreams. You of the Human Kingdom need to learn patience and acceptance. We can radiate the highest spiritual essence of these qualities at the same time that we express these qualities through our physical growth. When something is not right for you in your particular space, you can take action to change it, or you can become obstinate and rebellious. In Nature, our acceptance must be total, for there is no space for doubt or resistance to change. You can learn much about patience and acceptance by being with us through all the seasons.

In the Human Kingdom you learn to become more dependent upon others for love and self-worth. Therefore, your personal strength is tied to what outside life-force energies add to your own life-force energies. Sometimes you try to build your personal strength through competition. You even expand that particular concept to how Nature herself grows. That is totally incorrect, because competition is a wasteful use of life-force energies. We live in a cooperative manner because for us, Unconditional Love creates a completeness in our individuality. Therefore, we can teach you how to have an individual sense of self and at the same time be totally connected with the Divine Source.

—Grand Fir Deva

PAIN FROM HUMAN ACTIVITY

What is happening when you feel pain from a tree? There are many levels of energy that exist within all of Nature. When you attune with the highest spiritual levels of a tree, you will find Unconditional Love because that is what Nature truly expresses. When you tune into the level or frequency of individuality you find the patterns of memories that are stored within the energy consciousness of that particular tree. When those memories are painful you may sense grief, anger, pain, or some other perception of loss from the tree.

Each tree is harmonically connected with other members of its species and the bonding is particularly strong with trees in close proximity to each other. Thus when one member of the family becomes hurt, it is recorded within the other family members as well. It is like the grief that humans feel when a member of their family is lost. It is a sense of knowing what is happening in the physical form of one who is close to you. The more current the painful experience, the more pronounced is the discomfort that is projected from the tree.

If a tree has had a difficult growth cycle and then experiences a hurt to its own being, or the hurt to other members of its family, it may choose to close off communications with the Human Kingdom, and you may experience this as pain. When the tree has regained more of its life-force energy as it grows, it may be more willing to share with you.

When you ask permission from a tree to share with it, and receive a sense of pain, or a ''no'' answer, you must honor the space of the tree. You can reassure the tree that you were not part of the prior experience. It is then important to send Unconditional Love for the healing of its internal wounds, and then see the Unconditional Love going to all members of its species, and to the entire Planet. As you hold the image, you are giving Love back to the species, and all life benefits from this exchange of Unconditional Love.

There is a recognition by the tree that it cannot hold an imbalanced energy pattern indefinitely, in relationship to the Human Kingdom. At the higher levels of its being there is a willingness to have more harmony and Oneness with the Human Kingdom.

—*Western Red Cedar Deva*

ACCIDENTAL DEATH FROM
THE HUMAN KINGDOM

You ask me how I perceive the death of a tree when, for whatever reason, its needs have not been met by the Human Kingdom. We perceive the process where you interact with Nature as a learning process. At no time do we judge you for what you do with Nature. When a tree dies prematurely, and you feel guilt and pain as a result of your action or non-action, we first ask you to allow yourself the time and space to grieve for your loss. It is important to do this because holding onto your grief can block your pure connection with the trees when you wish further information about their needs. It is also important to take the time required to ask for love and forgiveness from the tree that has died, so that you can then love and forgive yourself. When you cannot unconditionally love yourself because of an experience that you have had, you restrict the process of learning that is so very important in the communication between Nature and Humankind. Next, you must ask yourself questions about what has happened, from a perspective of learning rather than judgement. Then you are prepared to take the appropriate actions for nurturing, as you plant another tree in the place of the tree that died.

Remember, beloved, that there is always a transference of energies that takes place between a tree that is dying and those life forms that are immediately in its environment, so that nothing is truly lost. Accept that you are moving into a more intimate relationship with Nature as a caretaker for Her life, and this will help ease your pain.

—*Douglas Fir Deva*

CHRISTMAS TREES

When a tree begins its growth cycle through the natural process, there is an immediate bonding with the Earth Element, and the other forms of life that support its being. When the process of germination and growth takes place through the Human Kingdom, the Consciousness of the tree is very much aware of human intentionality. When your intention is to plant the tree and cut it before it has completed its total cycle of being, that awareness is known to the tree. Therefore, the degree that a tree will commit itself to expanding to its fullest potential is held back from the Human Kingdom.

When the tree is to be cut, there is an awareness of the process about to happen, and life-force energy is diverted from the tree to other trees that are untouched by the Human Kingdom. Your intentionality when you cut a tree is also known to the tree. If you wish to have a Christmas tree because everyone else does, then you are not honoring the tree species itself. However, when you approach a tree with Unconditional Love and appreciation for its gifts, it will radiate Unconditional Love in the new space of your home.

If you wish to cut branches from the tree, it is important to attune with the tree itself, and ask for permission to take those branches. The particular branches may have a real life-force energy value in being part of the tree while it is with you.

After the tree has completed its purpose in being with you for the season, do not view it as a form of trash. It is better to place the tree in an outdoor setting where its life-force energy can be reabsorbed into the earth.

—*Overlighting Plant Deva*

LOGGING

Each tree species has its own purpose for growth on the planet. When you of the Human Kingdom make the choice to remove a particular species from its home, I tell you that you create an instability within the life-force energy system of the Planet. This instability is experienced by all Kingdoms, including your own. Your current relationship with Nature is based upon an economic structure of how much can be taken from Her, rather than a seeking of balance within Her. When you of the Human Kingdom speak about ''managing Nature,'' you must look at what you mean by managing. You must consider the effects of your actions on all life forms that are present in a given area. It is true that when you take from the Earth, you must give back to her in like kind. However, the time required for a tree that you plant to grow to maturity is not sufficient to restore the interrelationships of all the other life forms in that area. You must go beyond your emotions and thoughts to your deeper sensitivity, to truly understand the effects that your actions are having on all forms of life.

When a large area has been decimated, the life-force energy drops to a minimal level and then it is determined whether or not it is appropriate to rebuild the life-force energies there. If the area is going to be left alone by humans, steps may be taken to bring other life forms which germinate quickly to begin building the life-force energy in the area.

When you go into a natural space where cutting has taken place, you are encouraged to bless the land and the life forms present there. Bless what remains of the tree species themselves and affirm the energy transfer that is taking place to sustain and rebuild the life-force energies in the area. Give thanks to the trees that have been cut for the work that they have done. And finally, hold the vision of a continuity of life in that area. When you do this, you are helping Nature begin the process of restoring the life-force energies so that all species can fulfill their service in being on the Earth.

—Elder Grand Fir Deva

THE TRANSITION OF DEATH

Within the Human Kingdom, death is viewed with fear and anger as a completion, after which nothing takes place. Within the Kingdoms of Nature is the awareness that death is a transition in a continuing journey of experiences of many kinds. Death is known as an integral part of the physical life experience. When a leaf falls in the autumn, it is providing a space from which new life forms will be generated in a later season. When a tree loses a branch, there is a physical awareness of the event, and an acceptance that this condition is in the natural flow of things. When a tree dies in a forest fire it feels no pain, as you humans know it, for it perceives this event as part of a larger pattern of balance. When a tree dies of other natural causes, its life-force energy goes to other members of its family in the immediate area for their continued growth. The death transition becomes a shared experience and a bonding in Spirit with the Oneness of All Life. There is no pain, but rather a sense of fulfillment and completion that takes place within that species.

You of the Human Kingdom can learn much about the death transition from the Kingdoms of Nature. Do not hold onto life, and release your guilt and resentment about the transition that is taking place, whether it is your transition or that of another being. As you move into a greater acceptance of the transition process itself, you may come to see death as a space where you can be peaceful before moving on. Through the grieving process you learn to move from a space of separateness to a space of Oneness. Death becomes less painful as you learn non-attachment while you are still in a physical vehicle. Remember that the death transition is also another beginning within you, whether it is your own death or the death of a loved one.

—*Douglas Fir Deva*

DEATH AND THE EARTH CHANGES

There are indeed going to be changes within the physical structure of Planet Earth; however, do not fear for your own well-being. The transformation that is going to take place is a process of purification that will restore harmony, balance and positive evolution for all forms of life on this Planet. We support this process and ask that you do likewise with your own positive actions. Change is inevitable and as you of the Human Kingdom are more open to those changes, you will feel less apprehensive.

If you should choose to leave your physical body during this time of change, there are many ways that you can perceive this transition. First, you know that when you leave your physical form, you will be in a space where you can assist in the process of Earth balancing. You are going to understand what true power is from a spiritual perspective, and that physical strength is only one facet of power. Work needs to be done both on the physical Earth and in the spiritual world, so that your area of service will expand as you leave your body behind. I seek for you to see your own physical transition as the completion of one journey at the beginning of an even greater journey of service.

—Sequoia Deva

CHOICES

Every life form, including your own, requires pure water, air, earth and the beloved sun for it to grow and evolve on its particular path. You of the Human Kingdom have had an adverse impact on Planet Earth through the abuse of the resources that have been available to you for your conscious use. Planet Earth is now in a state where you can no longer separate your actions from their effect on the Earth Body. We can make changes to help restore balance, but the quality of energy of those actions is affected by what you do. We seek to work cooperatively with the Human Kingdom for the betterment of all life, and we ask you to make some difficult choices. You must choose whether the economic accumulation of goods, or the quality of life for all on this Planet, is to be your focus. In your daily activities, if you come upon an aspect of Nature that needs healing, be a responsible caretaker in that moment, in whatever way is available to you. You *do* make a difference when you act from a state of Pure Consciousness with your fellow humans and all forms of life.

The patterns of Consciousness that are set within the next few years are going to have a far-reaching impact on Planet Earth. We can no longer wait to initiate change for Her healing, and we welcome your support. Join us in the process of healing our Planet so that tomorrow may bring a time of blessedness and peace for all.

—Coastal Redwood Deva

NOTES

Chapter 1:
    1. Carl Sagan in a written appeal to the Global Forum of Spiritual and Parliamentary Leaders. National Resources Defense Council, *The Amicus Journal*, 12:3, Summer 1990, p. 53.
    2. Larry Ephron, *The End* (Berkeley, CA: Celestial Arts, 1988), p. 33.
    3. Chief Seattle's Testimony, a 1954 oration, cited in *The Extended Circle*, ed. Jon Wynne (Tyson Center Press, Fontwell Sussex, England, 1985).

Chapter 3:
    1. From *The Poetic Edda* (ca. A.D. 1200), quoted in Ralph Blum, *The Book of Runes* (New York: St. Martin's Press, 1987), p. 11.
    2. *Katha Upanishad* 6.1. The Sanskrit word for "fig tree," *asvattha*, comes from the word *asva* meaning "horse." Compare *Yggdrasil*, "Othin's steed," quoted in Joseph Campbell, *The Mythic Image* (Princeton, NJ: Princeton University Press, 1974), p. 192, and footnote p. 505.
    3. Liz and Colin Murray, *The Celtic Tree Oracle* (New York: St. Martin's Press, 1988), p. 88.
    4. *Black Elk Speaks: Being the Life Story of a Holy Man of the Oglala Sioux, as Told to John G. Neihardt* (New York: William Morrow and Co., 1932), quoted in Joseph Campbell, op. cit. p. 187.

Chapter 4:
    1. Paramahansa Yogananda, *Autobiography of a Yogi* (Los Angeles, CA: Self-Realization Fellowship, 1979), p. 411.
    2. Peter Tompkins and Christopher Bird, *The Secret Life of Plants* (New York: Harper and Row, 1973), p. 149.
    3. Yogananda, op. cit., p. 412.
    4. Richard St. Barbe Baker, *My Life—My Trees* (London, England: Lutterworth Press, 1970), p. 13.

5. The following Bach flower essences are made from tree flowers:
Aspen—Populus tremula
Beech—Fagus sylvatica
Cherry plum—Prunus cerasifera
Chestnut bud—Aesculus hippocastanum
Crab Apple—Malus pumila
Elm—Ulmus procera
Holly—Ilex aquifolium
Hornbeam—Carpinus betulus
Larch—Larix decidua
Oak—Quercus robur
Olive—Olea europa
Pine—Pinus sylvestris
Red Chestnut—Aesculus carnea
Sweet Chestnut—Castanea sativa
Walnut—Juglans regia
White Chestnut—Aesculum hippocastum
Willow—Salix vitellina
List of essences from Ellon Bach USA, Inc., 644 Merrick Road, Lynbrook, New York 11563.

6. Machaelle Small Wright, *Flower Essences* (Jeffersonton, VA: Perelandra Ltd., 1988), p. 16.

7. Ibid., p. 16.

Chapter 7:
1. In the bibliography you will find sources for making and ordering flower essences. This process is similar to that of making gem essences, which we describe in chapter six of our book, *The Newcastle Guide to Healing with Gemstones.*

Part Two, Introduction
1. George W.D. Symonds, *The Tree Identification Book* (New York: William Morrow & Company, 1958), p. 9.

BIBLIOGRAPHY

RESOURCES FOR TEXT

Bach, Edward, M.D. and F.J. Wheeler, M.D. *The Bach Flower Remedies*. New Canaan, Connecticut: Keats Publishing Inc., special contents copyright, 1977, 1979. Copyright 1931, 1933, 1952 by the Dr. Edward Bach Healing Centre. Published by arrangement with C.W. Daniel Company, Ltd., London. Original writings of Dr. Bach.

Blum, Ralph. *The Book of Runes*. New York, NY: St. Martin's Press, 1987. Poem and drawing of Odin hanging from the Yggdrasil tree.

Campbell, Joseph. *The Mythic Image*. Princeton, NJ: Princeton University Press, 1974. Discussion of trees in the mythology of ancient cultures.

Ephron, Larry. *The End*. Berkeley, CA: Celestial Arts, 1988. Explains John Hamaker's theory of the coming ice age and what we can do to stop it.

Frazer, James George. *The Golden Bough*. Garden City, NY: Doubleday, 1978. Describes the worship of trees in mythology and folklore.

Hall, Manly P. *The Mystical and Medical Philosophy of Paracelsus*. Los Angeles, California: The Philosophical Research Society, Inc., 1964. Gives a description of Paracelsus' beliefs about life-force energy, metaphysical healing, and the "Nature Spirits."

Hanley, Paul. "Richard St. Barbe Baker: Man of the Trees," *The Structuralist*. 23/24: 22–28, 1983–84. Informative article about Richard St. Barbe Baker, with photographs and quotes.

MacLean, Dorothy. *To Hear the Angels Sing*. Elgin, IL: Lorian Press, 1980. Dorothy MacLean's story of learning to communicate with the Devas.

Murray, Liz and Colin Murray. *The Celtic Tree Oracle*. New York, NY: St. Martin's Press, 1988. A Celtic divination tool with some fascinating information about the Celts.

Pilarski, Michael. "Reforesting the World," *The Light*. 1:7, pp. 20–21. August 1990. Comments on the need for reforestation.

Rosenblatt, Roger. "Introduction to Trees," *Life*. 13:7, pp. 28–30, May 1990. Documents the growing need for conservation.

Teale, Edwin Way. *Autumn Across America*. New York, NY: Dodd, Mead and Co. 1956. Appreciating Nature through the keen eyes of a naturalist. This book is one of a seasonal series.

Tompkins, Peter, and Christopher Bird. *The Secret Life of Plants*. New York, NY: Avon Books, 1973. A fascinating collection of experiments relating to the communication between plants and humans.

Tompkins, Peter, and Christopher Bird. *Secrets of the Soil*. New York, NY: Harper and Row, 1989. Focuses particularly on individual efforts to rebuild the soil from chemical damage, including the remineralization of trees.

Weeks, Nora. *The Medical Discoveries of Edward Bach, Physican*. New Canaan, Connecticut: Keats Publishing Inc., special contents copyright 1979. Copyright 1973 by the Dr. Edward Bach Healing Centre. Published by arrangement with C.W. Daniel Company, Ltd., London. A history of Dr. Bach's life and work.

Wright, Machaelle Small. *Flower Essences*. Jeffersonton, VA: Perelandra Ltd., 1988. All about the preparation and use of the Perelandra Flower Essences.

Yogananda, Paramahansa. *Autobiography of a Yogi*. Los Angeles, CA: Self-Realization Fellowship, 1979. Describes Yogananda's friendship with Luther Burbank.

TREE GUIDES

The following list is not meant to be a definitive list of tree guides and books about trees. These are the books that we chose to use on our particular travels and studies. We found our local library to be an excellent resource for guide books, as well as other books about trees.

Arno, Stephen. *Discovering Sierra Trees*. Published by the Yosemite Natural History Association and the Sequoia Natural History Association in cooperation with the National Park Service, U.S. Department of the Interior, 1973. Beautifully illustrated, informative guide for trees in the Sierra Nevada mountains in California.

Arno, Stephen and Ramona P. Hammerly. *Northwest Trees*. Seattle, Washington: The Mountaineers, 1977. A beautifully illustrated guide to Northwest trees.

Audubon Society. *Familiar Trees of North America, Western Region*. New York, NY: Alfred A. Knopf, Inc., 1986. Photographs are helpful in identifying Western trees.

Burnie, David. *Eyewitness Books: Tree*. New York, NY: Alfred A. Knopf, 1988. Beautiful color illustrations and clear text about the life cycle of a tree.

Common Trees of Pennsylvania. Published by the Commonwealth of Pennsylvania, Department of Environmental Resources, Harrisburg, PA, 1971. Good illustrations and text for the Eastern trees that are found in Pennsylvania.

Everchanging, Evergreen, the Lowland Forests of Olympic National Park. Published by the Olympic Branch, Pacific Northwest National Parks and Forests Assoc., in cooperation with Olympic National Park, 1984. Useful guide pamphlet to Northwest trees.

Fenton, Carroll Lane and Dorothy Constance Pallas. *Trees and Their World*. Eau Claire, Wisconsin: E.M. Hale and Company, 1962. Clear, simple text for children on the life cycle of a tree, with black and white drawings.

Hora, Bayard, ed. *The Oxford Encyclopedia of Trees of the World*. Oxford, England: Oxford University Press, 1981. Beautiful color photographs and drawings of ornamental trees and species from around the world.

Leathart, Scott. *Trees of the World*. New York, NY: A & W Publishers, 1977. Another beautifully photographed book of trees of the world.

Peattie, Donald Culross. *A Natural History of Western Trees*. Lincoln, Nebraska: University of Nebraska Press, 1953. A complete guide book, with good illustrations and lots of interesting information.

Petrides, George A. *A Field Guide to Trees and Shrubs*. Boston:

Houghton Mifflin Co., 1972. A useful, complete guide for identifying Eastern trees.

Platt, Rutherford. *A Pocket Guide to Trees, How to Identify and Enjoy Them*. New York, NY: Washington Square Press, 1960 (one of our tree guide books on which we relied heavily). The trees are organized by region, and good detail is given for identifying trees, along with other interesting information.

Symonds, George W.D. *The Tree Identification Book*. New York, NY: Quill, a division of William Morrow & Co., 1958. One of the best guide books that we have seen for Eastern trees. Beautiful black and white photographs.

Trees Every Boy and Girl Should Know. Published by the American Forestry Association, 919 17th St. N.W., Washington, D.C. 20006, 1968. An easy-to-read survey of trees across the country.

Walker, Laurence C. *Forests*. NY: Wiley & Sons, 1990. A naturalist's guidebook to trees and forest ecology.

Watts, Tom. *Pacific Coast Tree Finder*. Nature Study Guild, Box 972, Berkeley, CA 94701, 1973. Uses the key approach to tree identification, which is not especially easy, but it is interesting.

Zim, Herbert S., in consultation with the University of Colorado Museum Staff. *The Rocky Mountains*. New York, NY: Golden Press, 1964. A useful guide for touring the Rockies.

ADDITIONAL RESOURCES

Baker, Richard St. Barbe. *My Life, My Trees*. London, England: Lutterworth Press, 1970. Republished by Findhorn Press, Findhorn, Scotland, 1985.

Boone, J. Allen. *Kinship with All Life*. New York, NY: Harper & Row, 1954. Delightful and easily readable accounts of people, including the author, who have learned to communicate with Nature.

Bowden, Marcia. *Nature for the Very Young*. New York, NY: John Wiley & Sons, 1989. A handbook of indoor and outdoor activities for young children.

Cohen, Michael J., Ed.D. *How Nature Works*. Walpole, NH: Stillpoint Pub., 1988. How to regenerate a kinship with planet Earth.

Cornell, Joseph. *Sharing Nature with Children*. Nevada City, CA: Dawn Publications, 1979. A wealth of suggestions in highly readable form.

Cornell, Joseph. *Listening to Nature*. Nevada City, CA: Dawn Publications, 1987. Excellent book with beautiful photographs and inspirational poems on ways to appreciate Nature.

Cornell, Joseph. *Sharing the Joy of Nature*. Nevada City, CA: Dawn Publications, 1989. More nature activities for all ages.

Dreyer, Peter. *A Gardener Touched with Genius*. Berkeley, CA: University of California Press, 1985. A biography of Luther Burbank, one of the world's greatest plant breeders.

Ellon Bach U.S.A. Inc., P.O. Box 320, Woodmere, NY 11598. Source for the Bach Flower Remedies.

Ervin, Keith. *Fragile Majesty*. Seattle, WA: The Mountaineers, 1989. Describes the battle raging to save the Northwest forest.

Fairchild, Jill, ed. *Trees, A Celebration*. NY: Weidenfeld & Nicholson, 1989. A collection of poetry and other short works by authors who have loved trees.

Findhorn Community. *The Findhorn Garden*. New York, NY: Harper & Row, 1975. Describes in words and pictures the development of the Findhorn garden.

Hawken, Paul. *The Magic of Findhorn*. New York, NY: Bantam Books, 1975. An account of the founding and development of Findhorn.

Hecht, Suzanna and Alexander Cockburn. *The Fate of the Forest*. New York, NY: Routledge, Chapman & Hall, 1989. Tells the story of the rainforest of the Amazon river basin, past and present.

Kelly, David and Gary Braasch. *Secrets of the Old Growth Forest*. Salt Lake City, UT: Gibbs, Smith, Pub., 1988. A beautifully photographed book about the mismanagement and life-sustaining character of old growth.

Lipkis, Andy and Katie Lipkis. *The Simple Act of Planting a Tree*. Los Angeles, CA: Jeremy Tarcher, Inc. 1990. A workbook about how you can become a creator and keeper of an urban forest.

Lovelock, James. *The Ages of Gaia*. New York, NY: W.W. Norton & Co., 1988. A biography of our living earth.

Maser, Chris. *The Redesigned Forest*. San Pedro, CA: R & E Miles, 1988. A readable book about the importance of the old growth forest.

Moll, Gary and Sara Ebenrock, eds. for the American Forestry Association. *Shading Our Cities*. Covelo, CA: Island Press, 1989. A resource guide for urban and community forests.

Nollman, Jim. *Spiritual Ecology*. New York, NY: Bantam Books, 1990. Draws on Native American beliefs, shamanic perceptions, and the author's own experiences of communicating with animals, to show how we are interconnected with all life.

Orin Bridges. 6307 Hwy 2, Sandpoint, Idaho 83864. Notecards with photographs showing Devic energy around plants, animals and crystals.

Roads, Michael J. *Talking with Nature*. Tiburon, CA: H.J. Kramer Inc., 1987. Inspiring descriptions and channelings of sharing with Nature.

Roads, Michael J. *Journey into Nature*. Tiburon, CA: H.J. Kramer Inc., 1990. A continuation of Michael Roads' adventures with Nature.

Robbins, John. *Diet for a New America*. Walpole, NH: Stillpoint, 1987. A look at the inhumane conditions under which our animals for food production are raised. Emphasizes the interdependence of all life.

Robinson, Gordon. *The Forest and the Trees*. Washington, D.C.: Island Press, 1988. A guide to excellent forestry.

Rockwell, Sherwood and Williams. *Hug a Tree*. Mt. Rainier, MD: Gryphon House, 1983. Guided outdoor learning experiences for children.

Schneider, Stephen. *Global Warming*. San Francisco, CA: Sierra Club Books, 1989. Understanding climate change in terms of the global warming theory.

The Flower Essence Society, P.O. Box 459, Nevada City, CA, 95959. Source for the California Flower Remedies.

Van Gelder, Dora. *The Real World of Fairies*. Wheaton, IL: The Theosophical Publishing House, 1977. Colorful descriptions of author's perceptions of the Devas and the Nature Spirits.

Wright, Machaelle Small. *Behaving As If the God in All Life Mattered*. Jeffersonton, VA: Perelandra Ltd., 1983. A humorous and powerful account of how the Perelandra garden was co-created with the Devas and Nature Spirits.

Wright, Machaelle Small. *Garden Workbook*. Jeffersonton, VA: Perelandra, Ltd., 1987. How to go about planting a garden that is co-created with Nature.

SOME ENVIRONMENTAL MAGAZINES
AND NEWSLETTERS

Buzzworm, 1818 Sixteenth St., Boulder, CO 80302.

E Magazine, P.O. Box 6667, Syracuse, NY 13217.

Garbage Magazine, The Practical Journal for the Environment, P.O. Box 56519, Boulder, CO 80322.

Green Letter, Box 9242, Berkeley, CA 94709.

High Country News, P.O. Box 1090, Paonia, CO 81428.

In Context, P.O. Box 11470, Bainbridge Island, WA 98110.

Raise the Stakes, published by Planet Drum Foundation, Box 31251, San Francisco, CA 94131.

Soil Remineralization, A Network Newsletter, 152 South St., Northampton, MA 01060.

Tranet, The Transnational Network for Alternative/Appropriate Technology, Box 567, Rangely, ME 04970.

Whole Earth Review, 27 Gate Five Rd., Sausalito, CA 94965. Publisher of the Whole Earth catalogues.

ENVIRONMENTAL ORGANIZATIONS YOU CAN JOIN AND SUPPORT

Citizens for a Better Environment, Suite 505, 942 Market St., San Francisco, CA 94102.

Conservation International, 1015 18th St., N.W., Ste. 1002, Washington, D.C. 20036.

Co-op America, Dept. N.D., 2100 M. St., N.W., Washington, D.C. 20063.

Cultural Survival, 11 Divinity Ave., Cambridge, MA 02138.

EarthSave, P.O. Box 949, Felton, CA 95018-0949.

Earth First!, Box 5871, Tucson, AZ 85703.

Earth Island Institute, 300 Broadway, Suite 28, San Francisco, CA 94133.

Environmental Defense Fund, 1616 P St., N.W., Washington, D.C. 20036.

Environmental Policy Institute, 218 D St., S.E., Washington, D.C. 20003.

Environmental Protection Information Center, P.O. Box 397, Garberville, CA 95440.

Friends of the Ancient Forest, P.O. Box 3499, Eugene, Oregon, 97403.

Friends of the Earth, 530 7th St., S.E., Washington, D.C. 20003.

Friends of the Earth/UK, 2628 Underwood St., London, N17JU, England.

Friends of the Trees Society, P.O. Box 1064, Tonasket, WA 98855.

Global Tomorrow Coalition, 1325 G St., N.W., Ste. 915, Washington, D.C. 20005.

Greenpeace USA, 1611 Connecticut Ave., N.W., Washington, D.C. 20009.

Green Earth Foundation, Dept. ND, P.O. Box 1119, Fairfax, CA 94930.

Holyearth Foundation/Earthstewards Network, P.O. Box 10697, Bainbridge Island, WA 98110.

Institute for Food and Development Policy, 145 Ninth St., San Francisco, CA 94103.

International Union for Conservation of Nature and Natural Resources, Avenue du Mont-Blanc, Ch-1196 Gland, Switzerland.

International Wildlife Coalition, 1807 H. St., N.W., Suite 301, Washington, D.C. 20006.

National Arbor Day Foundation, 100 Arbor Ave., Nebraska City, NE 68410.

National Audubon Society, 645 Pennsylvania Ave., S.E., Washington, D.C. 20003.

National Coalition Against the Misuse of Pesticides, 530 7th St., Washington, D.C. 20003.

National Museum of Natural History, Smithsonian Institution, Washington, D.C. 20560.

National Resources Defense Council, 1350 New York Ave., N.W., Washington, D.C. 20005.

National Wildlife Federation, 1412 16th St., N.W., Washington, D.C. 20036.

National Zoological Park, Smithsonian Institution, Washington, D.C. 20008.

New England Tropical Forest Project, P.O. Box 73, Strafford, VT 05072.

New Forests Fund, 731 Eighth St., Washington, D.C. 20003.

People for a Future, 2140 Shattuck Ave., Berkeley, CA 94704.

Project LightHawk, P.O. Box 8163, Santa Fe, New Mexico 87504.

Rainforest Action Network, 300 Broadway, Ste. 28, San Francisco, CA 94133.

Rainforest Alliance, 320 Park Ave., 30th Floor, New York, NY 10022-6807.

Rainforest Echoes, P.O. Box B, Pago Pago, American Samoa, 96799.

Rainforest Foundation, P.O. Box 0101, Los Angeles, CA 90084.

Rainforest Health Alliance, In-house Division Project of Earth Island Institute, 300 Broadway, Ste. 28, San Francisco, CA 94133.

Rainforest Information Center, 1300 Park St., Santa Rosa, CA 95404.

Save-the-Redwoods League, 114 Sansome St., San Francisco, CA 94104.

Sierra Club, 730 Polk St., San Francisco, CA 94109.

Smithsonian Tropical Research Institute, APO Miami, Florida 34002-0011.

South Pacific Peoples Foundation of Canada, 409-620 View St., Victoria, B.C., Canada V8W 1J6.

Survival International, 2121 Decatur Place, N.W., Washington, D.C. 20008.

Terra International, P.O. Box 18391, Washington, D.C. 20036.

The Basic Foundation, P.O. Box 47012, St. Petersburg, FL 33743.

The Cousteau Society, 930 W. 21st St., Norfolk, VA 23517.

The Nature Conservancy, 1800 N. Kent St., Arlington, VA 22209.

The Wilderness Society, 1400 Eye St., N.W., Washington, D.C. 20005.

Threshold, P.O. Box 1856, Bisbee, AZ 85803.

TreePeople, 12601 Mulholland Drive, Beverly Hills, CA 90210. Directed by Andy and Katie Lipkis who wrote *The Simple Act of Planting a Tree.*

20/20 Vision, 69 South Pleasant, #203N, Amherst, MA 01002. Sends a monthly postcard on the most useful twenty-minute action that you can take at home.

World Resources Institute, 1735 New York Ave., Washington, D.C. 20006.

World Wildlife Fund/Conservation Foundation, 1250 214th St., N.W., Washington, D.C. 20006.

Worldwatch Institute, 1776 Massachusetts Ave., N.W., Washington, D.C. 20036.

NOTE

Please do not send us samples of leaves to identify. We are not botanists and cannot give you the kind of information that you seek. The best sources of information are knowledgeable people who live in your geographical area. Try those responsible for city landscaping, local nurseries that sell trees, nearby arboretums, the botany department at your local college or university, rangers at state parks, or the Department of Natural Resources at your state capital. If you live in a rural area it is possible that your local agricultural agent may be able to help you.

Bring with you a seed or cone as well as a fallen leaf for identification. The more information you have about the tree, the easier it will be to identify.